Engraving drawn by M. Bocourt

OXFORD IN ASIA
HISTORICAL REPRINTS
General Editor: JOHN BASTIN

HENRI MOUHOT'S DIARY

Drawn by M. H. Rousseau, from a Photograph.

HENRI MOUHOT

HENRI MOUHOT'S DIARY

TRAVELS IN
THE CENTRAL PARTS OF SIAM,
CAMBODIA AND LAOS
DURING THE YEARS 1858-61

ABRIDGED AND EDITED
BY CHRISTOPHER PYM

OXFORD
IN ASIA
Historical
Reprints

KUALA LUMPUR
OXFORD UNIVERSITY PRESS
LONDON   NEW YORK
1966

Oxford University Press, Ely House, London W.1.
GLASGOW NEW YORK TORONTO MELBOURNE WELLINGTON
CAPE TOWN SALISBURY IBADAN NAIROBI LUSAKA ADDIS ABABA
BOMBAY CALCUTTA MADRAS KARACHI LAHORE DACCA
KUALA LUMPUR HONG KONG
Bangunan Loke Yew, Kuala Lumpur
© *Oxford University Press* 1966

PRINTED BY CRAFTSMAN PRESS LTD SINGAPORE

CONTENTS

———

LIST OF PLATES

———

MAPS

———

ACKNOWLEDGEMENT

———

The Frontispiece and Endpapers (based on Mouhot's drawings) have been reproduced from the John Murray edition of Mouhot's diary (1864); the two route maps (Korat and Angkor) have been lent by the Royal Geographical Society; Mouhot's drawings (4 - 12), the facsimiles from his diary (1b, 2, and 3), and the Daguerreotype are provided by Mlle. Maud Mouhot, Mme. François Dellesmillières, and other members of Mouhot's family. The map to illustrate Mouhot's journeys has been drawn by F.W. Wentworth-Sheilds.

INTRODUCTION

——

HENRI Mouhot rediscovered the ancient Khmer civilization for the western world. He was the first explorer of the nineteenth century whose writings about the ruined Angkor Wat and Angkor Thom really fired people's imaginations. Previous explorers had mentioned the temples but their writings remained in obscurity. One of the reasons for the sudden worldwide interest in Mouhot's travels was Mouhot's own premature death in a remote part of Indochina. He died on the trail of more discoveries and was acclaimed posthumously. The means whereby he made known his astonishing finds was a chronicle of his journeys. This chronicle, the Mouhot diary which is here republished for the first time in a hundred years, was recovered from the forest where Mouhot died and brought back for the world to read.

The existence of Angkor was known to French missionaries who were Mouhot's guides and also known to certain Anglo-Saxon residents of Bangkok. One of these, the American missionary S.R. House, made notes about Angkor, but does not appear to have gone there himself. He was much interested in Cambodia and during the cholera epidemic of 1849 he treated a Cambodian prince who may have been his informant. In 1853 House journeyed to Korat in Siam where ancient Khmer ruins could be seen—thus anticipating Mouhot by eight years—but barely skirted Cambodia itself on the return journey.

D.O. King, an acquaintance of House, made a journey of exploration into Indochina in the years 1857-58. He wrote an account of Cambodia in a learned paper which was dispatched from America to the Royal Geographical Society of London in 1859. This paper was read at a meeting of the Society on 27 June 1859, the year before Mouhot visited Angkor. King's paper and the sketch-map which accompanied it were disappointing, but at the same meeting a second and more detailed paper was read. Its author, also an acquaintance of House, was a surgeon named Campbell. Later he made the acquaintance of Mouhot and helped him in various ways. Campbell's paper was compiled from the manuscripts of a traveller called E.F.J. Forrest and from information provided by House. This is what Campbell has to say about the most famous of all Khmer temples, Angkor Wat.

'[It] stands,' he writes, 'like a mighty sphinx frowning contemptuously on the infantine and barbaric state of the arts and science of the people who are now the denizens of the forests and plains in its vicinity, and presents, with its towers and halls so pregnant with mystery and evidence of the past, a wondrous enigma which challenges the wisdom of the world to fathom.'

By the time these words were read to members of the Royal Geographical Society Mouhot had already left London on the journey which would bring him fame. Neither the published accounts of Cambodia by King and Campbell, nor the mentions of Angkor in the writings of French missionaries, reached a wide public. But Mouhot's diary excited the civilized world. He did not claim any originality in rediscovering Angkor. His aim was, as he says, simply to disclose the existence of the temples.

Henri Mouhot, whose full name was Alexandre Henri Mouhot, was born at Montbéliard (Doubs) on 15 May 1826. The basic biographical material about him is to be found in the *Memoir of M. Henri Mouhot* by J.J. Belinfante which prefaced the 1864 book edition of his diary. Mouhot had three ambitions—to travel, to teach, and to study natural history. He was also interested in the recent discovery of photographic processes by Daguerre.

At the age of eighteen Mouhot went to Russia where he tutored the nobility in French and taught at a military academy. In his spare time he travelled to Poland and the Crimea taking photographs and making sketches of anything that interested him. Eventually after ten years' absence he returned to France. This was the year 1854 in which relations between France and Russia deteriorated and war broke out in the Crimea.

Belinfante says that Henri Mouhot and his brother Charles came to England in 1856 both having married relations of the African explorer Mungo Park. Henri's wife Anne, whom he calls 'Annette' in the letters, was proud of her connexion with Park, and she sometimes signed herself 'Anne Mouhot born Park'. Mungo Park came from a family of thirteen, and I have not yet established which of them was the father of Madame Mouhot. The newly-married Mouhots settled in Jersey where the desire to make a botanical expedition gradually took shape in Henri's mind. Finally his imagination is said to have been fired by an English book on Siam. It would be interesting to know which book, and I think it might have been Sir John Bowring's *The Kingdom and People of Siam* published in 1857.

With the thrilling examples of Mungo Park and other explorers before him Mouhot said goodbye to his wife and set off for the East. The diary is Mouhot's own account of journeys which lasted from 1858 until his death in 1861.

The explorer embarked at London in April 1858 and arrived in Siam four and a half months later. During the next three years he made four main expeditions from Bangkok into the interior of Indochina. His first journey which lasted from October until December 1858 took him northwards up the River Menam to a distance of about a hundred miles from Bangkok. He set out again at the end of December 1858 on a journey which lasted until April 1860.

On this second voyage Mouhot travelled by boat along the coast of Siam to Chantaboun which he used as a base for the first three months of 1859. He then continued his journey to Cambodia arriving at the port of Kampot. Travelling by land he went to Udong which he reached at the end of June, then spent most of July with the missionaries at their outpost in Pinhalu near Udong. In order to visit the primitive tribes in north-east Cambodia Mouhot hired a boat which took him down to Phnom Penh from Pinhalu and then up the River Mekong to a village beyond Kompong Cham and on the east bank. From here he travelled east by ox-cart towards the tribal plateau, but the rainy season made conditions so bad that he did not reach his destination—a distant missionary outpost at Brelum—until the middle of August. For three and a half months Mouhot stayed with missionaries as their guest and studied the tribes. At the end of November 1859 he retraced his steps and arrived back at Pinhalu a few days before Christmas. In January 1860 one of the missionaries from Battambang took Mouhot to Angkor where he spent three weeks studying the ruins. He then returned to Battambang and visited some more ancient Khmer sites. At the beginning of March 1860 he set off west by ox-cart and arrived in Bangkok a month later.

The third journey was an excursion from Bangkok to Pechaburi which lasted from May until August 1860.

Mouhot's fourth and last journey was obstructed by the temporary refusal of an official at Chaiapume to let him go northwards from Korat into Laos. Mouhot was obliged to return to Bangkok when he was already almost half way to Louang Prabang. Thus he covered the same ground between Bangkok and Korat four times. The first outward journey lasted from mid-October 1860 until the end of February 1861 at which time the explorer was turned back at Chaiapume. The journey to Bangkok and return to Chaiapume took another two months. Mouhot entered Laos by elephant in May 1861 and reached a village on the River Mekong at the end of June. The river was too dangerous for him to risk navigation so he continued by land to Louang Prabang where he arrived a month later. The last three months of his life (August, September and October 1861) were spent exploring the mountains and villages which surround Louang Prabang. He died on 10 November 1861.

In all these journeys Mouhot was accompanied by Asian servants six of whom he mentions by name. One of these, a Chinese youth called Phrai, played an important part. Mouhot recruited Phrai at Chantaboun during his second journey in 1859 and retained his services indefinitely. Phrai was with Mouhot when he died and rescued the diary. He, and another servant called Deng, brought back Mouhot's possessions from the forest and saved them for posterity.

It is perhaps ironic that the future French Indochina should have been explored by a Frenchman with English sponsors. Mouhot, a French Protestant with an English wife, found more encouragement in England than in France. In London he met those few Englishmen who had heard of Cambodia and knew a little about it. From Sir John Bowring's book a reader might discover that there was a vast palace in Cambodia near a huge lake. Readers of this book might also learn that the Cambodians thought their ancient palace had been built by the angels. Mouhot, the future rediscoverer of Angkor, may have known about the lost city and the myth of its angel-builders before he left England.

If he was diligent in his pursuit of knowledge—and Belinfante suggests he was — Mouhot could have discovered that the Cambodian king liked British goods. Beer brewed by a well-known English brewery was stored in warehouses at the Cambodian court. The Cambodian king possessed a coining machine made by Ingram of Birmingham. Cambodia was an unknown territory, but there was already some talk in London about a projected railway line from Rangoon to China with loop-lines to Cambodia and Tonking. However, maps of Cambodia did not mark Angkor, and the existence of ancient ruins there was not generally known.

Something must be said about the encouragement which Mouhot received from the Royal Geographical Society of Whitehall Place, London. The Society's charter indicated that geographical research was to be aided by the collection and publication of 'explorers' logs' —such as Mouhot's diary. A library was to be established together with a map room, for which purposes the Treasury gave an annual grant of five hundred pounds. A third purpose was to give information and suggestions to prospective explorers.

Mouhot was not backed financially by the Royal Geographical Society, nor was his widow successful in obtaining a pension from the Society after her husband's death. Henri Mouhot had saved up enough money to make his journey. But he would not have been justified in leaving wife and home if some interested persons had not encouraged him to continue with the project. The officers of the Royal Geographical Society helped Mouhot within the limits of their Society's charter.

The President of the Royal Geographical Society, Sir Roderick I. Murchison, went out of his way to help foreign travellers. He was a man of action and determined views. Once when J.S. Mill was fighting a parliamentary election Murchison remarked to a friend: 'I was out at eight o'clock to vote against him.' At Murchison's funeral Mr. Gladstone walked barefoot behind the coffin.

Murchison encouraged men like Mouhot to make their projected journeys to distant lands. Though he gave up being President of the Royal Geographical Society soon after Mouhot left England, he became President again in 1863—the year in which Mouhot's papers were being prepared for publication. Murchison probably read Mouhot's diary and recognized its merit.

Other fellows of the Royal Geographical Society were also helpful. John Arrowsmith of Hereford Square took on the task of arranging Mouhot's maps. Indochina was not unknown to Arrowsmith. In 1853 he had prepared a map of Burma with its adjacent countries and in 1858 he did a map of Siam with Annam. When

Arrowsmith had completed his work, the Mouhot maps were placed in the Map Room of the Royal Geographical Society where they may be seen today.

There are five letters from Mouhot's widow in the archives of the Royal Geographical Society, and I am grateful to the Librarian, Mr Crone, for allowing me to examine them. One of these letters, that which is dated 18 November 1862, throws light on the financial aspect of Mouhot's journey. Madame Mouhot, who was staying at 3a Hillmarton Villas, Camden Road, Holloway, addressed herself to Sir Roderick Murchison in the following terms:

'It may be necessary to inform you that Mr Mouhot's long continued labours were carried on entirely at his own expense and that he has in consequence left me without any other resources.'

She concluded her letter by asking Murchison for advice as to how she might pursue a claim for money. Shortly afterwards she wrote to the Secretary of the Royal Geographical Society saying she was in 'very straitened circumstances'. Although the Society was not enabled to grant Madame Mouhot a pension, Murchison probably used his influence with John Murray, the Society's publishers, to ensure that Mouhot's diary was at least published in a handsome edition.

Some more correspondence from Madame Mouhot exists in the archives of John Murray in London. Thanks to the kindness of Mr Simon Young I looked at these letters too. Madame Mouhot had wished an official French edition in book form to precede the English edition, but she was dissuaded. At first I thought that the official translator was Thomas Hodgkin, M.D., of Brook Street, Mayfair. Hodgkin had one important sympathy in common with Mouhot. Both men were passionate campaigners against slavery. Mouhot wrote an unpublished book on slavery in Russia. Hodgkin had written ferociously about the shabby links between slavery and the Free Traders. When at Mr Young's and my request John Murray kindly looked at his firm's ledgers he found an entry of

£62 paid to a G.K. Greville for translating. I assume that Hodgkin arranged the papers and G.K. Greville translated them.

On 30 April 1864 Madame Mouhot received the two volumes of diaries from John Murray. The next day she wrote to London saying how delighted she was with the result. The ledgers of John Murray reveal that the diary was published on a half profits agreement. A thousand copies were printed, and by 30 June 1871 there was still a deficit of £139.12.9. with 315 copies on hand. So the unfortunate widow made nothing out of the book. The French originals on which the book was based became the property of Mouhot's brother, Charles, and today they belong to his descendants. I am grateful to Mouhot's family, and in particular to the Countess Claude de Choiseul-Praslin for collating pages from the original diary and providing Mouhot's drawings for publication.

Now we come to Henri Mouhot's diary itself. There are three versions—the French magazine version (*Tour du Monde*, 1863, Nos 196-204), the English book version (*Travels in the Central Parts of Indo-china (Siam), Cambodia, and Laos*, 1864), and the French book version (*Voyage dans les Royaumes de Siam, de Cambodge, de Laos et autres parties centrales de l'Indochine*, 1868).

The 1863 version, which was edited to suit the needs of a magazine, was published by Hachette of Paris in nine consecutive instalments of *Tour du Monde*. These articles were illustrated with a series of lively engravings some of which were based on Mouhot's drawings. This collection of illustrations was to be used again in the English book version of 1864. I must mention in passing that the sixth instalment of *Tour du Monde* included a quotation from the book of an earlier traveller, the French missionary Bouillevaux. A certain controversy has raged ever since as to whether Mouhot or Bouillevaux was the true rediscoverer of Angkor. Certainly Bouillevaux visited Angkor and wrote about it before Mouhot, but so did other travellers.

The 1868 version was a French book edition of the *Tour du Monde*

articles. Once again Hachette was the publisher, and the editor was
Ferdinand de Lanoye. The initials 'F. de L.' had been published at
the foot of the final article in *Tour du Monde* No 204, so we may
presume that the same hand edited both the 1863 and 1868 versions.
In 1868 de Lanoye no longer mentioned the controversial name of
Bouillevaux which he had included in the earlier version of 1863.
This omission may have added fuel to the flames of what became
a futile controversy — Mouhot *versus* Bouillevaux — and which
need not concern us further.

The English book version of 1864 was approved by Mouhot's
family and carefully prepared for the press by John Murray of
London with advice forthcoming from the Royal Geographical
Society. I am satisfied that this is an authentic version of the diary.
The editors, who remained anonymous, chose their material from
Mouhot's manuscripts including the ten route maps on which the
explorer had scribbled important details. Relevant letters were also
included, together with such items of interest as Mouhot's meteoro-
logical readings, his versions of folk-tales, his Cambodian vocabu-
lary and a list of new discoveries in natural history. This material,
together with the *Tour du Monde* illustrations, covered more than
six hundred pages.

I have based my edition on the 1864 book version of John Murray.
I have transposed extracts from Mouhot's letters to positions in the
main text where they seemed appropriate, and noted briefly where
this has been done. I have also transposed a section of the diary
itself (the first paragraph of Chapter Seven), but otherwise my
chief editorial tasks have been to cut the diary's length and to
introduce new chapter headings. I have not interfered with the
spelling of proper names except with several very well-known
names e.g. 'Touli-Sap' and 'Penom-Peuh'. In these instances the
editors clearly mistook Mouhot's 'n' for 'u', so I have made the
necessary corrections. Twice I have restored measurements where
those in the 1864 version were ridiculous—e.g. the height of the

balustrade at Angkor Wat. The index is intended to help readers marry the nineteenth century and present-day spelling of place names.

There are no new writings of Henri Mouhot in this volume. All has been published previously. However, the publishers may claim the originality of publishing for the first time Mouhot's own drawings (on which the nineteenth-century engravings were based), two of his route maps and pages from the diary itself. This brief introduction of mine replaces the Dedication and Preface by Charles Mouhot which with the Memoir by J.J. Belinfante preceded the 1864 version. I have taken some of my facts from Charles Mouhot and Belinfante as well as drawing on unpublished material. I doubt whether Mouhot's life is itself worth a full-length book, but I heard recently that two more books are projected—a biography by a French author and a historical novel based on Mouhot's life by an American author. I welcome this renewal of interest in the subject.

Although Mouhot is remembered today for rediscovering Angkor, the avowed purpose of his Indochina travels was natural history. Explorers who followed in his footsteps were offered insects by the local inhabitants who believed that entomology must be the chief enterprise of European travellers. Mouhot's specimens were shipped back to England and sent to experts who wrote reports. It is worth recalling what some of these experts wrote at the time.

On 16 August 1860 Lovell Reeve, an Essex conchologist, wrote a letter in which he compared the hitherto unknown shell of Mouhot *Helix Mouhoti* (later renamed *Helix Cambojiensis*) with the known shell *Helix Brookei*. The main difference was in the lower half of the whorls—Mouhot's shell being white and Brooke's being dark chestnut. Dr Gray, one of the editors of a scientific magazine, published a short account of Mouhot's tortoises three of which were too young for him to identify—though later he did identify one of them. A Portuguese professor of botany praised Mouhot's insects as important additions to the coleopterous fauna of Indochina. One of Mouhot's spiders was pronounced 'so extraordinary that we have not hesitated to refer it to a new genus'.

My own chief interest in Mouhot is the journey to Cambodia, but before leaving Indochina I also fulfilled a long-standing ambition to visit his tomb in Laos. I started from Phnom Penh, the capital of Cambodia, travelled by road to Paksé in south Laos, then flew to Louang Prabang by way of Vientiane. Both the Laotian authorities and some American missionaries assured me that monuments raised in memory of famous Frenchmen had been removed since Laos obtained its independence. Undeterred by these reports and knowing where to look for Mouhot's tomb I set off from Louang Prabang one Christmas morning and in less than five hours I walked to Mouhot's tomb, examined it and returned to Louang Prabang in time to eat Christmas dinner with my hosts.

The route lay along the banks of the Nam Khan, a tributary of the Mekong. After about two hours' walk I asked a villager from Ba Peunom where the grave was and came directly to it lying between my path and the river. The tomb erected by Auguste Pavie was visible in a forest clearing. With no difficulty I reached the tomb itself and bent down to read the inscription:

H. MOUHOT

Naturaliste

1829-1867

The dates of this inscription puzzled me for I remembered that Mouhot died in 1861—six years earlier than Pavie seemed to have thought. On my return to Phnom Penh I discovered the cause of the mistake—and also incidentally that I was not the first to notice it.

Mouhot's first tomb was erected by the explorers, Doudart de Lagrée and Garnier, in 1867. Instead of recording the dates of

Mouhot's life, de Lagrée put up a plaque bearing the inscription 'H. MOUHOT—Mai 1867'. A second tomb was constructed by Dr. Neis in 1883, and a third tomb—the existing one—in 1887. Pavie erroneously took the date of the first tomb copied on the second tomb as the date of Mouhot's death.

In a letter Doudart de Lagrée referred to Mouhot as 'an excellent man of whom I find memories everywhere'. In the course of reading the literature of Indochina exploration I have found these sentiments repeated many times. Henri Mouhot found his vocation in the forests of Indochina. The way in which he describes his travels reveals a man at peace with himself. He writes that his chief interest was natural history. His diary is republished today because of the great Khmer civilization whose ruined temples he rediscovered.

London,   CHRISTOPHER PYM
July 1965

I

SIAM

On the 27th April, 1858, I embarked at London, in a sailing ship of very modest pretensions, in order to put in execution my long-cherished project of exploring the kingdoms of Siam, Cambodia, and Laos, and visiting the tribes who occupy the banks of the great river Mekon.

I spare the reader the details of the voyage and of my life on board ship, and shall merely state that there were annoyances in plenty, both as regards the accommodation for the passengers and the conduct of the captain, whose sobriety was more than doubtful.

We arrived at Singapore on the 3rd September. I made only a short stay there, my chief object being to gain information respecting the country I was about to visit. On the 12th of the same month, after a very monotonous voyage, we arrived at the mouth of the river Menam, on whose banks Bangkok is built. A vast sandbank here bars the entrance of large ships, and compels them to go eight or nine miles farther up the gulf, and discharge their cargoes at great additional expense. Our vessel, however, only drawing eight feet of water, passed without much difficulty, and anchored at Paknam in front of the Governor's house, whither the captain and myself proceeded without loss of time, in order to obtain the necessary permission to continue our route.

This formality over, I hastened to visit the forts, which are of brick and battlemented, the markets, and some of the streets. Paknam is the Sebastopol or Cronstadt of the Kings of Siam; nevertheless, I fancied that a European squadron could easily master it, and that the commander, after breakfasting there, might dine the same day at Bangkok.

On a little island in the middle of the river rises a famous and rather remarkable pagoda, containing, I was told, the bodies of their last kings. The effect of this pyramidal structure reflected in the deep and limpid water, with its background of tropical verdure, was most striking.

The Menam deserves its beautiful name—Mother of Waters— for its depth permits the largest vessels to coast along its banks without danger: so closely, indeed, that the birds may be heard singing gaily in the overhanging branches, and the hum of numberless insects enlivens the deck by night and day. The whole effect is picturesque and beautiful. Here and there houses are dotted about on either bank, and numerous villages give variety to the distant landscape.

We met a great number of canoes managed with incredible dexterity by men and women, and often even by children, who are here early familiarised with the water. I saw the Governor's children, almost infants, throw themselves into the river, and swim and dive like waterfowl. It was a curious and interesting sight, particularly from the strong contrast between the little ones and the adults. Here, as in the whole plain of Siam, which I afterwards visited, I met most attractive children, tempting one to stop and caress them; but as they grow older they rapidly lose all beauty, the habit of chewing the betel-nut producing an unsightly blackening of the teeth and swelling of the lips.

Bangkok is the Venice of the East, and whether bent on business or pleasure you must go by water. In place of the noise of carriages and horses, nothing is heard but the dip of oars, the songs of sailors, or the cries of the Cipayes (Siamese rowers). The river is the high street and the boulevard, while the canals are the cross streets, along which you glide, lying luxuriously at the bottom of your canoe.

We cast anchor in front of the cathedral of the French Mission and of the modest palace of Monseigneur Pallegoix, the worthy archbishop, who, for nearly thirty years, without any assistance but that of missionaries as devoted as himself, has made the revered

4

emblem of Christianity and the name of France respected in these distant regions.

The sight of the Cross in foreign lands speaks to the heart like meeting with an old friend; one feels comforted and no longer alone. It is beautiful to see the devotion, self-denial, and courage of these poor and pious missionaries; a blessing as they are, also, to travellers, it would be ungrateful not to render them the gratitude which is their just due.

During a ten years' residence in Russia I witnessed the frightful effects of despotism and slavery. In Siam, results not less sad and deplorable obtruded themselves on my notice; every inferior crouches before a higher in rank; he receives his orders kneeling, or with some other sign of abject submission and respect. The whole of society is in a state of prostration.

I was making my preparations for departure on the 16th October, my purpose being to penetrate into the north of the country and visit Cambodia and the savage tribes belonging to it, when I received an invitation from the King of Siam to be present at the great dinner which this monarch gives every year, on his birthday, to the European residents in Bangkok. I was presented by Monseigneur Pallegoix, and his Majesty's reception was kind and courteous. His costume consisted of a pair of large trousers, a short brown jacket of some thin material, and slippers; on his head he wore a little copper helmet like those worn by the naval officers, and at his side a rich sabre.

Most of the Europeans in Bangkok were present at the dinner, and enthusiastic toasts were drunk to the health of his Majesty, who, instead of being seated, stood or walked round the table, chewing betel and addressing some pleasant observation to each of his guests in turn. The repast was served in a vast hall, from whence we could see a platoon of the royal guard, with flags and drums, drawn up in the courtyard. When I went to take leave of the King, he graciously presented me with a little bag of green silk, containing some of the gold and silver coin of the country—a courtesy which was most unexpected, and for which I expressed my gratitude.

A singular institution, peculiar to Siam, Cambodia, and Laos, exists in a second king, slightly inferior to the other, and having a sort of reflected authority, the limits of which are not easily defined. His official title is Wangna, a word which literally signifies 'the youngest King'. He has his court, his mandarins, and his little army, and they pay him royal honours; but in reality he is merely the first subject of his colleague. His sole prerogative is exemption from the customary prostration before the King, instead of which he salutes him by raising both hands in the air. It is true, he is allowed to draw largely from the royal treasury, but never without an order from the King, which, however, is rarely refused.

After my visits of ceremony to the two kings, I hastened to finish the preparations for my voyage. I bought a light boat capable of holding all my chests, reserving a narrow space for myself, and another for the bipeds and quadrupeds forming my adopted family —viz., two rowers, one of whom also officiated as cook, a parroquet, an ape, and a dog. One of the boatmen was a Cambodian, and the other an Annamite, both Christians, and knowing a few words of Latin and English, so that, as I had already picked up a little Siamese, I could make myself pretty well understood. Latin is much esteemed among the native Christians, thanks to the ritual of the Catholic mission.

On the 19th October I quitted Bangkok, and commenced my voyage up the Menam. The current runs very strongly at this season, and it took us five days to go about seventy miles. At night we suffered terribly from the mosquitoes, and even during the day had to keep up the incessant fanning to drive off these pestilent little vampires. They were so numerous that you could catch them by handfuls, and their humming resembled that of a hive of bees. These insects are the curse of all tropical countries, but here they peculiarly abound in the marshes and lands covered with slime and mud left by the retiring waters, where the heat of the sun and the moisture combined, favour their rapid increase. My legs suffered especially from their attacks.

As the country was entirely inundated, we could not land anywhere, and even after killing a bird I frequently could not get at it. All this was very tantalising, for the banks of the stream are very gay and attractive, nature wearing here her richest dress.

On arriving at Ayuthia, my rowers conducted me direct to the excellent Father Larmandy, a French missionary, by whom I was expected. The good priest received me with great kindness, and placed at my disposal all he had to offer in his little house. He employs his leisure time in the study of natural history and in hunting, and frequently accompanied me in my rambles. As we explored the woods we talked of our own charming country—France.

After a long hunting or rowing expedition, we always, on our return home, found our repast prepared by my servant Niou, who excelled in Siamese cookery, and which our fatigue made us doubly appreciate. Rice and omelette, or curried fish, bamboo-stalks, haricots, and other wild vegetables, formed our diet, with the addition of roast fowls and game when the chase had been fortunate.

The heat was sometimes overwhelming; for a week we had 90 degrees of Fahrenheit in the shade throughout the twenty-four hours, but the mosquitoes were fewer in number, which was a great relief. In our excursions we visited some ruins amid the woods, and I made a collection of beautiful butterflies, and found several insects new to me.

I drank nothing but tea, hoping by abstinence from cold water and from all wine and spirits, to escape fever. So far, my health had certainly never been better, not even in the north of Russia. The people flocked to see my collections, and could not imagine what I should do with so many animals and insects. I used to amuse myself by offering the children my cigar-ends to smoke, in return for which they would run after butterflies, and bring them to me uninjured.

I discovered here a sort of spider, which is also, I believe, found at the Cape, from which a silken thread may be drawn out by taking hold of the end hanging from its body. One has but to go on winding; the thread is very strong, and never breaks.

It requires some time to become accustomed to the shrill chirpings during the night of myriads of grass-hoppers and other insects, which seem never to sleep. There appears to be no such thing as silence or repose; everywhere is a continual stir, the gushing overflow of life in this exuberant region.

What a contrast between the subdued tints and cold skies of Europe, and this burning clime and glittering firmament! How pleasant it was to rise in the early morning before the glowing sun had begun its course; and sweeter still in the evening to listen to the thousand sounds, the sharp and metallic cries, which seemed as though an army of goldsmiths were at work!

On the 13th November we arrived at a village called Arajik, where the land was more elevated. Here I killed several white squirrels, animals which I had not met with in the neighbourhood of Bangkok. It is only in the solitude and depth of the woods that one can fully admire and enter into the sort of harmony and concord which reigns in the songs of the various birds, forming such a pleasing kind of symphony that the voice of one is rarely over-powered by that of another; one can enjoy at once the general effect and the melodious note of the particular winged musician we prefer. Scarcely does the sun begin to gild the tops of the trees, when, alert and gay, they commence their morning hymn. The martins, the warblers, the drongos, and the dominicans, respond to the turtle-doves' cooing in the highest branches. Music of a less dulcet nature is discoursed by the aquatic and rapacious tribes, such as cranes, herons, and kingfishers, who from time to time utter their piercing cries.

I procured a guide in the mandarin of the village, who received me courteously, and offered me, in return for some trifling presents, a breakfast of rice, fish, and bananas. I requested his aid in arranging my purposed visit to Mount Phrabat, a favourite object of pilgrimage among the Siamese, who resort thither yearly in great numbers to adore the sacred footprint of Buddha. He volunteered to accompany me, an offer which I gratefully accepted.

After staying a week on the mountain, and adding many pretty and interesting objects to my collection, our party returned to Arajik, the Prince of Phrabat insisting on sending another guide with me, although my friend the mandarin, with his attendants and elephants, had kindly remained to escort me back to his village. There I again partook of his hospitality, and, taking leave of him the day following, I resumed my voyage up the river. Before night I arrived at Saraburi, the chief town of the province of Pakpriau, and the residence of the governor.

Saraburi is a place of some extent, the population consisting chiefly of Siamese, Chinese, and Laotian agriculturists; and consists, like all towns and villages in Siam, of houses constructed of bamboo. They peep out, half hidden among the foliage along the banks of the river; beyond are rice-plantations, and, farther in the background, extensive forests, inhabited solely by wild animals.

On the morning of the 26th we passed Pakpriau, near which the cataracts begin. The waters were still high, and we had much trouble to fight against the current. A little to the north of this town I met with a poor family of Laotian Christians, of whom the good Father Larmandy had spoken to me. We moored our boat near their house, hoping that it would remain in safety while I explored the mountains in the neighbourhood, and visited Patawi, which is the resort of the Laotian pilgrims, as Phrabat is of the Siamese.

All the country from the banks of the river to the hills, a distance of about eight or nine miles, and the whole surface of this mountain range, is covered with brown iron-ore and aerolites; where they occur in the greatest abundance, vegetation is scanty and consists principally of bamboo, but it is rich and varied in those places where the detritus has formed a thicker surface of soil. The dense forests are infested with leopards, tigers, and tiger-cats. Two dogs and a pig were carried off from the immediate vicinity of the hut of the Christian guardians of our boat during our stay at Pakpriau; but the following day I had the pleasure of making the offending leopard pay for the robbery with his life, and his skin served me for a mat.

Where the soil is damp and sandy I found numerous traces of these animals, but those of the royal tiger are more uncommon. During the night the inhabitants dare not venture out of doors; but in the day-time the creatures, satisfied with the fruits of their predatory rambles, skulk into their dens in the recesses of the woods. One day I went to explore the eastern part of the chain of Pakpriau, and, becoming excited in the chase of a wild boar, we soon lost ourselves in the forest. The animal made his way through the brushwood much more easily than we could—encumbered as we were with guns, hatchets, and boxes—and we ere long missed the scent. By the terrified cries of the monkeys we knew we could not be far from some tiger or leopard, doubtless, like ourselves, in

search of prey; and, as night was drawing in, it became necessary
to retrace our steps homeward for fear of some disagreeable adven-
ture. With all our efforts, however, we could not find the path.
We were far from the border of the forest, and were forced to
take up our abode in a tree, among the branches of which we made
a sort of hammock. On the following morning we regained the
river.

I endeavoured fruitlessly to obtain oxen or elephants to carry
our baggage with a view of exploring the country, but all beasts
of burden were in use for the rice-harvest. I therefore left my boat,
and we set off, like pilgrims, on foot for Patawi on a fine morning
with a somewhat cloudy sky, which recalled to me the pleasant
autumn days of my own country. We followed for three hours,
through forests infested with wild beasts, the road to Korat, and
at last reached Patawi.

I went to the extreme north of the mount, where some generous
being has kindly had constructed, for the shelter of travellers, a
hall, such as is found in many places near pagodas. The view here
is indescribably splendid, and I cannot pretend to do justice either
with pen or pencil to the grand scenes which here and elsewhere
were displayed before my eyes. I can but seize the general effect
and some of the details; all I can promise to do is to introduce
nothing which I have not seen. Hitherto all the views I had seen
in Siam had been limited in extent, but here the beauty of the
country is exhibited in all its splendour. Beneath my feet was a
rich and velvety carpet of brilliant and varied colours; an immense
tract of forest, amidst which the fields of rice and the unwooded
spots appeared like little streaks of green; beyond, the ground, rising
gradually, swells into hills of different elevations; farther still to
the north and east, in the form of a semicircle, is the mountain-chain
of Phrabat and that of the kingdom of Muang-Lom; and in the

extreme distance those of Korat, fully sixty miles distant. All these join one another, and are, in fact, but a single range.

At the sight of this unexpected panorama a cry of admiration burst simultaneously from all mouths. Even my poor companions, generally insensible to the beauties of nature, experienced a moment of ecstacy at the sublimity of the scene. 'Oh! *di, di*' (beautiful), cried my young Laotian guide; and when I asked Kue what he thought of it, 'Oh! master,' he replied, in his mixed jargon of Latin, English, and Siamese, 'the Siamese see Buddha on a stone, and do not see God in these grand things. I am pleased to have been to Patawi.'

About ten o'clock on the second night of my stay the dogs suddenly began to utter plaintive howls. 'A tiger! a tiger!' cried my Laotian, who was lying near me. I started up, seized my gun, and half-opened the door; but the profound darkness made it impossible to see anything, or to go out without uselessly exposing myself. I therefore contented myself with firing off my gun to frighten the creature. The next morning we found one of our dogs gone.

We scoured the neighbourhood for about a week, and then set off once more by water for Bangkok, as I wished to put my collections in order and send them off.

The places which two months previously had been deep in water were now dry; and everywhere, around their dwellings, the people were digging their gardens and beginning to plant vegetables. The horrible mosquitoes had reappeared in greater swarms than ever, and I pitied my poor servants, who, after rowing all day, could obtain no rest at night. Luckily we had no longer to contend with the current, and our boat, though heavily laden, proceeded rapidly.

We were about three hours' sail from Bangkok, when I perceived a couple of European boats, and in a room built for travellers near a pagoda I recognized three English captains of my acquaintance, one of whom had brought me to Singapore. They were, with their wives, enjoying a picnic, and, on seeing me, insisted on my joining them and partaking of the repast.

I reached Bangkok the same day, and was still uncertain as to a lodging, when M. Wilson, the courteous Danish Consul, came to me, and kindly offered the hospitality of his magnificent house.

I consider the part of the country which I had just passed through, extremely healthy, except, perhaps, during the rains. It appears that in this season the water, flowing down from the mountains and passing over a quantity of poisonous detritus, becomes impregnated with mineral substances, gives out pestilential miasmata, and causes the terrible jungle-fever, which, if it does not at once carry off the victim, leaves behind it years of suffering. My journey, as has been seen, took place at the end of the rainy season and when the floods were subsiding; some deleterious exhalations, doubtless, still escaped, and I saw several natives attacked with intermittent fever, but I had not had an hour's illness. Ought I to attribute this immunity to the regimen I observed and which had been strongly recommended to me—abstinence, all but total, from wine and spirits, and drinking only tea, never cold water? I think so; and I believe by such a course one is in no great danger.

II

JOURNEY TO CAMBODIA

My intention now was to visit Cambodia, but for this purpose my little river-boat was of no use. The only way of going to Chanta-boun was by embarking in one of the small Chinese junks or fishing-vessels, which I accordingly did on the 28th December, taking with me a new servant called Nion, a native of Annam, and who, having been brought up at the college of the Catholic priests at Bangkok, knew French well enough to be very useful to me as an interpreter. The boat was inconveniently small, and we were far from comfortable; for, besides myself and servant, there were on board two men, and two children about thirteen. I was much pleased with the picturesque aspect of all the little islands in the gulf; but our voyage was far longer than we expected, three days being its usual duration, while owing to a strong head-wind it occupied us for eight.

On the night of the 31st December our boat was making rapid way under the influence of a violent wind. I was seated on the little roof of leaves and interlaced bamboos which formed a sort of protection to me against the rain and cold night-air, bidding adieu to the departing year and welcoming in the new one; praying that it might be a fortunate one for me, and, above all, that it might be full of blessings for all those dear to me. The night was dark; we were but two miles from land, and the mountains loomed black in the distance. The sea alone was brilliant with that phosphoric light so familiar to all voyagers on the deep. For a couple of hours we had been followed by two sharks, who left behind them a luminous and waving track. All was silent in our boat; nothing was to be heard but the wind whistling among the rigging and the rushing of the waves; and I felt at that midnight hour—alone, and far from all I loved—a sadness which I vainly tried to shake off, and a disquietude which I could not account for. Suddenly we felt a violent shock, immediately followed by a second, and then the vessel remained stationary. Every one cried out in alarm; the sailors rushed forward; in a moment the sail was furled and torches lighted, but, sad to say, one of our number did not answer to his name. One of the young boys, who had been asleep on deck, had been thrown into the sea by the shock. Uselessly we looked for the poor lad, whose body doubtless became the prey of the sharks. Fortunately for us, only one side of the boat had touched the rock, and it had then run aground on the sand; so that after getting it off we were able to anchor not far from the shore.

On the 3rd January, 1859, after having crossed the little gulf of Chantaboun, the sea being at the time very rough, we came in sight of the famous Lion rock, which stands out like the extremity of a cape at the entrance of this port. From a distance it resembles a lion couchant, and it is difficult to believe that Nature unassisted has formed this singular Colossus. The Siamese—a superstitious race—hold this stone in great veneration, as they do everything that appears to them extraordinary or marvellous. It is said that the captain of an English ship, once anchored in the port, seeing the lion, proposed to buy it, and that, on the governor of the place refusing the offer, he pitilessly fired all his guns at *the poor animal*. This has been recorded in Siamese verse, with a touching complaint against the cruelty of the Western barbarians.

On the 4th January, at eight o'clock in the morning, we arrived at the town of Chantaboun, which stands on the bank of the river, six or seven miles from the mountain range. The missionaries at Bangkok having given me a letter of introduction to their fellow-labourer at Chantaboun, I had the pleasure of making acquaintance with the worthy man, who received me with great cordiality, and placed at my disposal a room in his modest habitation. I passed sixteen days, very agreeably, with him, sometimes hunting on Mount Sabab, at other times making excursions on the rivers and canals. The country greatly resembles the province of Pakpriau, the plain being, perhaps, still more desert and uncultivated; but at the foot of the mountains, and in some of the delightful valleys, pepper is grown in some quantity by the Chinese.

I bought, for twenty-five ticals, a small boat to enable me to visit the isles of the gulf. The first I landed at was named Konam-Sao; it is in the form of a cone, and nearly 250 metres in height, but only two miles in circumference. Like all the other islands in this part of the gulf, it is of volcanic origin. The rocks which surround it make the access difficult; but the effect produced by the richness and bright green of the vegetation is charming. The dry season, so agreeable for European travelling, from the freshness of the nights and mornings, is in Siam a time of stagnation and death for all nature; the birds fly to the neighbourhood of houses, or to the banks of the rivers, which furnish them with nourishment; rarely does their song come to enchant the listener; and the fishing-eagle alone utters his hoarse and piercing cry every time the wind changes. Ants swarm everywhere, and appear to be, with the mosquitoes and crickets, the only insects that have escaped destruction.

Nowhere did I find in these islands the slightest trace of path or stream; and it was extremely difficult to advance at all through the masses of wild vine and interwoven branches. I was forced to make my way, hatchet in hand, and returned at night exhausted with the heat and fatigue.

On the 26th we set sail for the first of the Ko-Man islands, for there are three, situated close together, bearing this name. The largest is only twelve miles from the coast. Some fishing-eagles, a few black doves, and a kind of white pigeon were the only winged creatures I saw. Iguanas are numerous, and when in the evening they come out of their retreats, they make such a noise in walking heavily over the dead leaves and branches, that one might suppose it caused by animals of a much larger size.

Toward evening, the tide having fallen, I allowed my boat to ground on the mud, which I had remarked during the day to be like a peat-bog impregnated with volcanic matter; and during the whole night so strong a sulphureous odour escaped from it, that I imagined myself to be over a submarine volcano.

On the 28th we passed on to the second island, which is higher and more picturesque than the other. The rocks which surround it give it a magnificent effect, especially in a bright sunlight, when the tide is low. The isles of the Patates owe their name to the numerous wild tubers found there.

I passed several days at Cape Liant, part of the time being occupied in exploring the many adjacent islands. Two years ago, when the king visited Chantaboun, they built for him on the shore, at the extremity of the cape, a house and kiosk, and, in memory of the event, they also erected on the top of the mountain a small tower, from which a very extensive view may be enjoyed.

I also made acquaintance with Ko-Kram, the most beautiful and the largest of all the islands north of the gulf between Bangkok and Chantaboun. The whole island consists of a wooded mountain-range, easy of access, and containing much oligist iron.

On the morning of the 29th, at sunrise, the breeze lessened, and when we were about three miles from the strait which separates the isle of Arec from that of the 'Cerfs', it ceased altogether. For the last half-hour we were indebted solely to our oars for the little progress made, being exposed to all the glare of a burning sun; and the atmosphere was heavy and suffocating. All of a sudden, to my great astonishment, the water began to be agitated, and our light boat was tossed about by the waves. I knew not what to think, and was seriously alarmed, when our pilot called out, 'Look how the sea boils!' Turning in the direction indicated, I beheld the sea really in a state of ebullition, and very shortly afterwards an immense jet of water and steam, which lasted for several minutes, was thrown into the air. I had never witnessed before such a pheno-menon, and was now no longer astonished at the powerful smell of sulphur which had nearly overpowered me in Ko-Man. It was really a submarine volcano, which burst out more than a mile from the place where we had anchored three days before.

On March 1st we reached Ven-Ven, at Paknam-Ven, the name of the place where the branches of the river unite. This river, whose width at the mouth is above three miles, is formed by the union of several streams flowing from the mountains, as well as by an auxiliary of the Chantaboun river, which, serving as a canal, unites these two places. Ascending the stream for fourteen or fifteen miles, a large village is reached, called Bandiana, but Paknam-Ven is only inhabited by five families of Chinese fishermen.

Crocodiles are more numerous in the river at Paknam-Ven than in that of Chantaboun. I continually saw them throw themselves from the banks into the water; and it has frequently happened that careless fishers, or persons who have imprudently fallen asleep on the shore, have become their prey, or have afterwards died of the wounds inflicted by them. This latter has happened twice during my stay here. It is amusing, however—for one is interested in observing the habits of animals all over the world—to see the manner in which these creatures catch the apes, which sometimes take a fancy to play with them. Close to the bank lies the crocodile, his body in the water, and only his capacious mouth above the surface, ready to seize anything that may come within reach. A troop of apes catch sight of him, seem to consult together, approach little by little, and commence their frolics, by turns actors and spectators. One of the most active or most impudent jumps from branch to branch till within a respectful distance of the crocodile, when, hanging by one claw, and with the dexterity peculiar to these animals, he advances and retires, now giving his enemy a blow with his paw, at another time only pretending to do so. The other apes, enjoying the fun, evidently wish to take a part in it; but the other branches being too high, they form a sort of chain by laying hold of each other's paws, and thus swing backwards and forwards, while any one of them who comes within reach of the crocodile torments him to the best of his ability. Sometimes the terrible jaws suddenly close, but not upon the audacious ape, who just escapes; then there are cries of exultation from the tormentors, who gambol about joyfully. Occasionally, however, the claw is entrapped, and the victim dragged with the rapidity of lightning beneath the water, when the whole troop disperse, groaning and shrieking. The misadventure does not, however, prevent their recommencing the game a few days afterwards.

On the 4th I returned to Chantaboun from my excursions in the gulf, and resumed charge of my collections, which, during my absence, I had left at the Custom-house, and which, to my great satisfaction, had been taken good care of. The tide was low, and we could not go up to the town. The sea here is steadily receding from the coast, and, if some remedy be not found, in a few years the river will not be navigable even for boats. Already the junks have some trouble in reaching Chantaboun even at high water. The inhabitants were fishing for crabs and mussels on the sandbanks close to the Customs-house, the *employés* in which were occupied in the same pursuit. The chief official, who, probably hoping for some small present, had come out to meet me, heard me promise a supply of pins and needles to those who would bring me shells, and encouraged his men to look for them. In consequence, a large number were brought me, which, to obtain otherwise, would have cost much time and trouble.

Here I am, once more installed in the house of a good old Chinese, a pepper-planter, whose hospitality I enjoyed on my first visit to the place, two months ago. His name is Ihié-How, but in Siamese he is called Apait, which means *uncle*. He is a widower with two sons, the eldest eighteen, a good young man, lively, hardworking, brave, and persevering. He is already much attached to me, and is desirous of accompanying me to Cambodia. Born amidst the mountains, and naturally intelligent, there are none of the quadrupeds and few of the feathered tribes found in the district with whose habits he is not familiar. He fears neither tiger nor elephant. All this, added to his amiable disposition, made Phrai (that is his name) a real treasure to me.

I had cut my heel in climbing the rocks on the shore at Ko-Man, and, as I was constantly barefooted in the salt water, the wound soon closed. But afterwards I began to suffer from it; my foot swelled, and I was obliged to re-open the wound to extract a piece of shell which had remained in it. Apait has resigned to me his bed, if that can be so styled, which consists merely of a few laths of areca placed upon four stakes. I have extended my mat upon this framework, and should enjoy uninterrupted sleep all night were it not for the swarms of ants which frequently disturb me by passing over my body, getting under my clothes and into my beard, and, I almost fancy, would end by dragging me out, if I did not from time to time, shake them off. Occasionally great spiders and other disgusting creatures, crawling about under the roof, would startle me by dropping suddenly on my face.

At the entrance of Apait's garden, in front of his house, I had made a kind of shed with stakes and branches of trees, covered with a roof of leaves, where I dried and prepared my large specimens, such as the long-armed apes, kids, and horn-bills, as also my collections of insects. It is very agreeable, after a fatiguing day's chase over hills and amongst dense forests, through which one must cut one's way axe in hand, to repose in the evening on the good Chinaman's bench in front of his house, shaded by bananas, cocoanut, and other trees. The worthy old Apait has at last consented to allow his son to enter my service, provided I pay him thirty ticals, half a year's wages in advance. This will enable him, if he can sell his house and pepper-field, to clear off his debt and retire to another part of the mountain. Phrai is delighted to attend me, and to run about the woods all day, and I am not less pleased with our bargain, for his knowledge of the country, his activity, his intelligence, and attachment to me, are invaluable.

The rainy season is drawing near, storms become more and more frequent, and the growling of the thunder is frightful. Insects are in greater numbers, and the ants, which are now looking out for a shelter, invade the dwellings, and are a perfect pest to my collections, not to speak of myself and my clothes. Several of my books and maps have been almost devoured in one night. Fortunately there are no mosquitoes, but to make up for this there is a small species of leech, which when it rains quits the streams and infests the woods, rendering an excursion there, if not impracticable, at all events very disagreeable. You have constantly to be pulling them off you by dozens, but, as some always escape observation, you are sure to return home covered with blood; often my white trousers are dyed as red as those of a French soldier.

The royal and other tigers abound here; every night they prowl about in the vicinity of the houses, and in the mornings we can see the print of their large claws in the sand and in the clay near streams. By day they retire to the mountain, where they lurk in close and inaccessible thickets. Now and then you may get near enough to one to have a shot at him, but generally, unless suffering from hunger, they fly at the approach of man. A few days ago I saw a young Chinese who had nineteen wounds on his body made by one of these animals; he was looking out from a tree about nine feet high, when the cries of a young kid, tied to another tree at a short distance, attracted a large tiger. The young man fired at it, but, though mortally wounded, the creature, collecting all his strength for a final spring, leaped on his enemy, seized him and pulled him down, tearing his flesh frightfully with teeth and claws as they rolled on the ground. Luckily for the unfortunate Chinese, it was a dying effort, and in a few moments more the tiger relaxed its hold and breathed its last.

The fruit here is exquisite, particularly the mango, the mangus-teen, the pine-apple, so fragrant and melting in the mouth, and, what is superior to anything I ever imagined or tasted, the famous 'durian', which justly merits the title of king of fruits. But to enjoy it thoroughly one must have time to overcome the disgust at first inspired by its smell, which is so strong that I could not stay in the same place with it. On first tasting it I thought it like the flesh of some animal in a state of putrefaction, but after four or five trials I found the aroma exquisite. By an odd freak of nature, not only is there the first repugnance to it to overcome, but if you eat it often, though with ever so great moderation, you find yourself next day covered with blotches, as if attacked with measles, so heating is its nature.

A few days ago I made up my mind to penetrate into a grotto on Mount Sabab, half-way between Chantaboun and Kombau, so deep, I am told, that it extends to the top of the mountain. I set out, accompanied by Phrai and Niou, furnished with all that was necessary for our excursion. On reaching the entrance of the grotto we lighted our torches, and, after scaling a number of blocks of granite, began our march. Thousands of bats, roused by the lights, commenced flying round and round us, flapping our faces with their wings, and extinguishing our torches every minute. Phrai walked first, trying the ground with a lance which he held; but we had scarcely proceeded a hundred paces when he threw himself back upon me with every mark of terror, crying out, 'A serpent! go back!' As he spoke I perceived an enormous boa about fifteen feet off, with erect head and open mouth, ready to dart upon him. My gun being loaded, one barrel with two bullets, the other with shot, I took aim and fired off both at once. We were immediately enveloped in a thick cloud of smoke, and could see nothing, but prudently beat an instant retreat. We waited anxiously for some time at the entrance of the grotto, prepared to do battle with our enemy should he present himself; but he did not appear. My guide now boldly lighted a torch, and, furnished with my gun reloaded and a long rope, went in again alone. We held one end of the rope, that at the least signal we might fly to his assistance. For some minutes, which appeared terribly long, our anxiety was extreme, but equally great were our relief and gratification when we saw him approach, drawing after him the rope, to which was attached an immense boa. The head of the reptile had been shattered by my fire, and his death had been instantaneous, but we sought to penetrate no farther into the grotto.

I know not to what it is to be attributed, unless it be the pure air of the mountains and a more active life, but the mountaineers of Chantaboun appear a much finer race than the Siamese of the plain, more robust, and of a darker complexion. Their features, also, are more regular, and I should imagine that they sprang rather from the Arian than from the Mongolian race. They remind me of the Siamese and Laotians whom I met with in the mountains of Pakpriau. Will the present movement of the nations of Europe towards the East result in good by introducing into these lands the blessings of our civilization? or shall we, as blind instruments of boundless ambition, come hither as a scourge, to add to their present miseries?

I quitted with regret these beautiful mountains, where I had passed so many happy hours with the poor but hospitable inhabitants. They accompanied me to a great distance, begging me not to forget them, and to pay them another visit. I made an agreement with some pagan Annamite fishermen to give them thirty ticals for taking me from Chantaboun to Komput, a province of Cambodia. We arrived in the harbour at seven in the evening, and were detained there for two days by a contrary wind, too violent to allow us to leave without danger. Two days later we reached Ko-Khut, where, again, pouring rain and a head wind compelled us to anchor about 100 metres from the shore in a small bay which was far from promising much security to our little craft.

Our position was not agreeable; our frail bark, rudely tossed by the furious waves, seemed every moment in danger of being dashed upon the rocks. Our baggage, to which we had assigned the best place for preservation from wet, occupied three-fourths of the boat, and we were crowded five of us together in the bows, with no better shelter than some palm-leaves sewn together, through which the water dripped, and kept us continually soaked. The rain falling without intermission, we could not keep the fire alight to cook our rice, and for four days remained half-lying in the boat, scarcely able to move in the narrow space left for us, and our clothes clinging to us with wet. At last, on the fifth day, we had the pleasure of seeing the sky clear up and the wind change. About two o'clock in the afternoon, foreseeing a fine night, and having revived the drooping courage of my men by a stiff dose of arrack, we weighed anchor and left Ko-Khut with a fair breeze.

It was quite a comfort to be able to move and breathe freely, and I spent a part of the night under my little awning of palm-leaves, enjoying the beauty of the heavens and the rapid movement of the vessel. At daybreak we perceived, about ten miles distant, the first of the islands of Koh-Kong. It is smaller than Koh-Chang, and neither so imposing in general appearance nor having such a splendid range of peaked hills. The island is nearly a desert, but it produces the beautiful cardamom, as also gamboge, collected from the bamboos, which the natives split open when hard.

I soon forgot the miseries of the first part of our voyage, and was amply recompensed by the shifting scenes of beauty presented to us by the group of islands we were passing. At length we reached the advanced posts of the pirates of Komput, from the heights of which they keep a look-out, and, as soon as a sail comes in sight, make preparations for an attack. We had no cause for fear, having no merchandise to tempt them; and, moreover, we were all well armed. About five in the evening we cast anchor in a little bay, where we cooked our rice, and my men lay down to take some repose, having had none the night previous. We were a day and a half's sail from Komput, and at midnight we resumed our voyage, gently rocked by the waves and favoured by a light breeze.

After passing the island of Phu-Quoc, which belongs to Cochin-China, the view became more and more beautiful; land surrounded us on all sides, and we seemed to be sailing on a lake. The scenery in this gulf is truly enchanting. Eastward extend the coast and islands of Cochin-China as far as Ita Jienne, and to the north and west are those of Cambodia, crowned by a mountain 900 metres in height, which is so like Sabab that Phrai called out to the pilot, 'You are taking us back to Chantaboun; there is Mount Sabab.' We were not, however, long permitted to enjoy the splendid picture here displayed before us, for very shortly after our entrance into the gulf large black clouds, gathering at the summit of the mountain, by degrees hid it entirely from view, the thunder growled, and a terrific wind arose, which hurried our boat along at an extraordinary rate. The pilot at the helm shook all over, and begged for arrack to sustain his strength and courage. When the storm had lasted half an hour a heavy rain began to descend, and with it the wind moderated. We had now arrived at the mouth of the river on which Komput is situated.

III

MEETING WITH
THE CAMBODIAN KING

It happened to be the day fixed for the King of Cambodia, then in Komput, to pass in review all the ships lying in the roads; but for some time he had been detained by the rough weather in a sort of apartment erected for him on piles, in a place where the water was shallow. As we passed the Custom-house, we perceived the royal *cortège* advancing towards a large junk, which his Majesty was having built as a trading-vessel for Singapore.

The river leading to Komput is about 300 metres in width, but rising in the neighbouring mountains, its course is but very limited. Though Komput is now the only port of Cambodia, it is far from being as full of life and bustle as Bangkok, for the town boasts only 300 houses at most, and a population scarcely equal to that of Chantaboun. All its little commerce is supplied by Lower Cochin-China, the ports of which are almost always closed against Europeans, so that rice, which is imported in a sort of contraband manner, some tons of gamboge, a little ivory, fish taken in the lake by the Annamites, a small quantity of cotton, and valuable wood, constitute the whole of the commerce of the town; and I venture to predict that, when the ports of Annam are thrown open to Europeans, the Chinese merchants will abandon Komput altogether. And yet, under a better system of government, this country might supply a great number of articles, of which I will speak hereafter. It will not probably be long before what remains of this unfortunate land will fall under the dominion of some other power. Possibly, France has her eyes fixed upon it, with the view of annexing it to her possessions in Lower Cochin-China.

After having sailed up the pretty river for about a mile, we came in sight of a house covered with creepers, and surmounted by a cross, which indicated the residence of the Abbé Hestrest, the head of the foreign mission here. Reader, have you journeyed in foreign lands? Have you ever for a time, more or less long, been separated from your friends and relatives—shut out from civilised society? Have you been tossed about by tempests or buffeted by your fellow-men? Have you narrowly escaped some great danger? Have you been unhappy? Have you lost some one very dear to you? In one word, have you *suffered*? If you have, you will apreciate the feelings with which the solitary wanderer welcomes the divine cross, the heart-stirring emblem of his religion. It is to him a friend, a consoler, a father, a brother; at sight of it the soul expands, and the more you have suffered the better you will love it. You kneel down, you pray, you forget your griefs, and you feel that God is with you. This is what I did.

I had letters to the Abbé Hestrest from several of the missionaries in Siam. We therefore anchored, and I landed; but the nine days' inactivity to which I had been forced to submit had so cramped my limbs, that for a time I had almost lost the use of them, and could scarcely walk. The abbé received me like a brother, and offered me accommodation in his humble abode until I could find lodgings elsewhere. The first piece of news which he imparted to me was, that France was at war with Austria. I did not even know that there had been a difference between the two Governments.

Scarcely had I landed when the return of the king from his aquatic excursion was announced. The Abbé Hestrest conducted me to the banks of the river; and as soon as his Majesty perceived a stranger by the side of the priest, he gave orders to his rowers to approach the shore, and, when within hail, addressed the abbé:

'Who is the stranger with you?'

'Sire, a Frenchman,' replied my companion.

'A Frenchman?' repeated the king, quickly. Then turning to me, 'You are French?'

'Yes, sire,' I answered in Siamese.

34

'Monsieur comes from Paris,' said the abbé; 'but he has recently visited Siam.'

'And what does he come to my kingdom for?'

'He has a particular mission, which has nothing to do with politics; it is merely to see the country. M. Mouhot will soon wait upon your majesty.'

After a few minutes' silence, the king, waving his hand, and saying '*Au revoir,*' passed on.

I was at first afraid that the abbé had made me pass for a less humble and modest individual than I really was, and I should be forbidden the kingdom. The very name of France is full of dread to these poor monarchs; and this present one lived in daily fear of seeing the French flag waving in the roads. He is about sixty years of age, short and stout. He wears his hair cut rather close, and his countenance is good-natured, mild, and intelligent.

The king was reclining on a thick cushion in the stern of his boat, which was of European build. Four rowers and a dozen young girls were with him; and among the latter I remarked one, whose features were delicate and pretty, dressed in the European style, and wearing long hair. She would have been reckoned a pretty girl anywhere, and was, I fancy, the favourite, for she was in a richer costume than the others, and covered with jewels. She also occupied the place nearest the king, and seemed to pay great attention to her old adorer. The rest were fat, with bloated faces and vulgar features, and had their teeth blackened by betel and arrack. Besides a kind of petticoat, the corners of which are looped up and fastened to the sash behind, some wore a tight jacket, white or blue, buttoning over the chest; and had a red scarf, which, according to the custom of the Siamese and Cambodian women, was passed round the body under the arms, and tied at the bosom.

Some days after my arrival I was installed in a house built by the king's orders, and at his own expense, for the accommodation of European merchants, who, however, do not often visit Komput. The king was expecting a visit from me, and had sent several persons to find out who I was; his idea being, that I was an officer of the French army in Cochin-China, despatched from thence to gain information about the country. I begged M. Hestrest to accompany me to see the king; for which purpose we proceeded a mile and a half up the river to Kompong-Bay, which is the Cambodian part of the town, and the residence of the governor, and where his Majesty and suite were encamped.

When we arrived he was holding a kind of levée, in a building constructed of bamboo with some elegance, and covered with red cloth, but the interior of which looked more like a theatre than a royal abode. Finding at the door neither sentinel nor porter, we entered without being announced. The king was seated on an old European chair, with two officers on each side of him, who from time to time offered him, kneeling, a lighted cigarette, or some betel, which they kept always ready. At a little distance stood his guards, some holding pikes ornamented at the top with white tufts; others with sheathed sabres in their hands. The ministers and mandarins knelt a few steps below his Majesty. On our entrance, chairs similar to the king's were placed for us close to him. Like his subjects, he generally wears nothing but the *langouti*, the native dress. His was composed of yellow silk, confined at the waist by a magnificent belt of gold studded with precious stones. At Cambodia, as at Siam, it is necessary to offer presents, if one desires to gain the royal favour. I had accordingly brought with me an English walking-stick gun, as a gift for the king. It at once attracted his notice.

'Pray show me that cane,' he said, in Cambodian.

I gave it to him.

'Is it loaded?' asked he, seeing it was a fire-arm.

36

'No, sire.'

He then begged for a cap and snapped it; unscrewed the barrel and examined it with great attention.

'If it would be agreeable to his Majesty,' I said to M. Hestrest, 'I shall be happy to offer it to the king.'

The abbé interpreted my words.

'What did it cost?' asked the king.

'Sire, I dare not ask M. Mouhot. In Europe no one tells the price of what he gives.'

The king then begged to look at my watch, and, after inspecting it attentively, again asked the price. The abbé then alluded to my design of visiting Udong, the capital of Cambodia, and of journeying through the country.

'Go to Udong; go about,' said the king, laughing. 'Very well.'

He then asked my name, and tried to write it; on which I drew out my pocket-book and gave him one of my cards. He seemed to wish for the pocket-book, and I presented him with it.

'Sire,' said M. Hestrest, 'as M. Mouhot is going to Udong, perhaps your Majesty will deign to facilitate his journey.'

'Willingly. How many carriages do you want?'

'Three will be sufficient, sire.'

'And for what day?'

'The day after to-morrow, sire.'

'Take a note of that, and give orders about it,' said the king to his secretary. He then rose, and shaking hands with us, retired. We returned to our hotel. I say hotel, for it is the only lodging for strangers; and M. de Montigny, when ambassador at Komput, lived there, indications of which were afforded by the inscriptions scratched on the walls by the sailors belonging to the expedition, such as 'Hotel of the king and ambassadors'; 'Here is lodging for man, horse and elephant gratis pro Deo'; 'Good beds, sofas, and dining-tables on the floor'; 'Sea-water bathing—in the river'; 'Good table—in the market'; 'Good wine—at Singapore'; 'Nothing—for the servants'.

All my preparations for departure having been completed, the Abbé Hestrest came on the morning of the day fixed, to invite me to breakfast with him; after which he offered to take me in his own boat to Kompong-Bay, where the promised vehicles were to meet us.

When we arrived there, none were to be seen. We applied to the first mandarin, who, chewing his betel, displayed his black teeth with a stupid grin, and I then perceived that I had been duped by these people, who are always and everywhere false; never yielding but to force, and holding the very name of a European in detestation. After various complaints, and remonstrances with the the mandarins, we with great difficulty obtained three carriages, by courtesy so called; but the dog-cars in use in Holland would have been more serviceable to me; so I sent back the three wheel-barrows to the king, with my compliments, and hired other vehicles for myself.

Udong, the present capital of Cambodia, is situated north-east of Komput, and is four miles and a half from that arm of the Mekon which forms the great lake, lying about 135 miles from Komput as the crow flies. It is reckoned an eight-days' journey, travelling with oxen or buffaloes, and there are eight stations on the way. With elephants you can accomplish it in half the time; but only the king, the mandarins, and very wealthy persons can afford these animals. The conveyances which I had engaged could scarcely hold my baggage, so that my men were obliged to make the journey on foot.

Perceiving in the shops several necklaces, bracelets, and rings formed of a material like jet, I inquired from whence it was procured, and was told that it came from the neighbouring island of Phu Quoc, where it was to be found in abundance. I afterwards handled a piece of this substance, and discovered it to be a sort of coal. It would burn well in a lamp, and greatly resembles the cannel coal of Scotland.

After traversing a marshy plain, where we knocked down several aquatic birds, we entered a beautiful forest, which stretches unbroken to the very gates of Udong. To cross this marsh I had to put on my hunting-boots, which I had not worn for some time, and consequently the leather had hardened so much, that, after two hours' walking in the heat of the day, the skin was rubbed off my feet in several places; and I was forced to take off the boots and continue my journey barefoot. Luckily, owing to the dry weather and the constant communication between Komput and the capital, the road was almost everywhere in good condition. The heat was intense, and our progress excessively slow; but at length we reached the first station, where I was lodged in a large hall, thatched and built of bamboo, which had been erected for the accommodation of the king and his suite. At night, guards were stationed at my door to protect me from robbery; and, thanks to the royal letter which I carried, I was respectfully treated. On the following morning I managed, at the cost of a franc of our money, to hire an elephant to take me as far as the next station.

From thence I continued my route barefoot, and our sufferings from the heat exceeded all I had ever imagined of the effect of the sun in the torrid zone. Its burning rays, falling on the sandy soil, became intolerable at ten o'clock in the morning, so that even the natives, the soles of whose feet were much harder than mine, could not bear contact with the bare ground, but sought for tufts of grass to step upon. The oxen could scarcely move, and showed every sign of pain and exhaustion; and, in spite of spurring and blows,

39

often refused to stir. The water in the ponds was not warm, but literally hot; the whole atmosphere seemed on fire, and all nature languishing and prostrate. At ten o'clock we halted until three. We sadly felt the want of drinkable water, as also did our cattle, which suffered from thirst even more than ourselves. To make our tea and cook our rice, we had no resource but the stagnant pools, impregnated with unwholesome matter by the vomica-nuts which fall from the surrounding trees.

The day following I was fortunate enough to obtain another elephant; but after this there was no more help to be met with, and the greater part of the ensuing four days' journey I performed on foot, my attendants contriving to perch themselves on the corners of one of the waggons. At this dry season a broad track in the middle of the road, which altogether is from twenty-five to thirty metres in width, is beaten hard by the frequent passage of vehicles and elephants, and the fine thick dust arising from it is very annoying. The remainder of the road is covered with grass and shrubs, and on either hand is the forest, with its trees tall, straight, and majestic, surmounted by immense tufts of leaves. The effect is that of a magnificent avenue; and from the regularity of the intervals between the trees, one might almost believe that it had been laid out by the hand of art.

The stations are equidistant from each other, about twelve miles apart; and at all of them, besides the old caravanserais for the shelter of ordinary travellers, new ones, much more spacious and ornamental, have been erected for the accommodation of the king. There are also intermediate resting-places between every two stations, where travellers can obtain a welcome shelter from the midday heat.

On leaving Komput a low chain of hills came in sight on our left hand, but everywhere on our route we met with the same sandy soil, except in a single spot, which was stony, and contained veins of iron-ore. We passed through but one village, and there, only, were a few attempts at cultivation. In no other part of the forest could I distinguish any traces of its being inhabited. On approaching the capital, the prospect became more diversified; we passed fields of rice, cottages encircled by fruit-gardens, and country houses belonging to the Cambodian aristocracy, who come here in the evening for the sake of breathing a purer air than they can find in the city. As we drew closer to the gates I found the place to be protected by a large moat, surmounted by a parapet, and enclosed by a palisade three metres high. I expected to enter a fortified town, and to be received by a sentinel with fixed bayonet, and with the startling words, 'You cannot pass'. But seeing no one, I pushed open the gate and entered.

IV

UDONG

IT seemed that I was in the enclosure surrounding the palace of the second king. The first object that attracted my attention was a sort of cage, something between a sentry-box and a pigeon-house, with a small window at each of the four sides, intended for a look-out house and signal-station in case of invasion. I then found myself in the centre of a large square surrounded by ramparts, and the access to which is by two gates, one opening on the market-place, and the other on the country. Within this walled space is, on one side, the palace of the inferior king, and opposite are the residence of a younger prince, his brother, and a pagoda. All these buildings were thatched.

I hoped to find here, as at Komput, an 'Hotel for the king and ambassadors', but, not seeing any sign hung out, I bent my steps to a house where many persons were passing in and out. It was the hall of justice, and the judges were then sitting. I sent my man Niou to ask if they would give shelter to a traveller, and had not long to wait for an answer, for both judges and accused came out to see me, and I was brought into the hall, where I was an object of great curiosity, all crowding round me and asking me what I sold.

The news of my arrival soon reached the ears of the king, and two pages were sent to request me to wait at once on his Majesty; but my luggage was not yet forthcoming, and I objected that I could not visit him in my travelling-dress. 'Oh, that is nothing; the king has no dress at all, and he will be delighted to see you,' was the reply. Scarcely had my waggons arrived when a chamberlain, followed by a page, came to say that the king was waiting for me. I went, therefore, to the palace, before the entrance of which were a dozen dismounted cannon, in whose mouths the sparrows had built their nests. Further off a crowd of vultures were devouring the remains from the table of the king and his courtiers. I was ushered into the audience-chamber, which communicates with his Majesty's private apartments, and is paved with large Chinese tiles, the walls being whitened with chalk. A number of Siamese pages, fine young men from twenty-five to thirty years of age, uniformly dressed in a *langouti* of red silk, were standing in groups, or seated in Oriental fashion, waiting the king's appearance. A few minutes after my arrival he entered, and every forehead was bowed to the ground. I rose, and he advanced towards me, with an air at once easy and distinguished.

'Sire,' said I, 'I had the honour of an interview with the first King at Komput, and of being favoured by him with permission to visit Udong.'

'Are you French or English?' he asked, examining me attentively.

'I am a Frenchman, Sire.'

'You are not a merchant; why do you come to Cambodia?'

'Sire, I came through Siam to see your country, and to hunt here, if allowed.'

'Very good. You have been in Siam? I also have visited Bangkok. Come and see me again.'

'As often as my presence will be agreeable to your Majesty.'

After a few more minutes' conversation, the king held out to me his hand, which I kissed, and I then retired; but had not proceeded far when several officials ran after me, exclaiming, 'The king is enchanted with you; he wants to see you often.'

The following day I devoted to making an investigation of the city. The houses are built of bamboos or planks, and the marketplace, occupied by the Chinese, is as dirty as all the others of which I have made mention. The longest street, or rather the only one, is a mile in length; and in the environs reside the agriculturists, as well as the mandarins and other Government officers. The entire population numbers about 12,000 souls.

The many Cambodians living in the immediate vicinity, and, still more, the number of chiefs who resort to Udong for business or pleasure, or are passing through it on their way from one province to another, contribute to give animation to this capital. Every moment I met mandarins, either borne in litters or on foot, followed by a crowd of slaves carrying various articles; some, yellow or scarlet parasols, more or less large according to the rank of the person; others, boxes with betel. I also encountered horsemen, mounted on pretty, spirited little animals, richly caparisoned and covered with bells, ambling along, while a troop of attendants, covered with dust and sweltering with heat, ran after them. Light carts, drawn by a couple of small oxen, trotting along rapidly and noisily, were here and there to be seen. Occasionally a large elephant passed majestically by. On this side were numerous processions to the pagoda, marching to the sound of music; there, again, was a band of ecclesiastics in single file, seeking alms, draped in their yellow cloaks, and with the holy vessels on their backs.

The third day after my arrival at Udong the court of justice was noisily opened at eight o'clock in the morning; and the loud voices of the judges and advocates were still resounding through the hall at five in the afternoon, having never for an instant been hushed, when suddenly two pages came out of the court of the palace, crying out, 'The King!' A thunderbolt falling in the hall could not have caused a greater sensation than this announcement; there was a general hurryscurry; judges, advocates, accused, and spectators fled pell-mell, taking refuge in the corners with their faces to the ground. I laughed to see the legal functionaries, and the Chinamen with their long queues, rushing against each other in their eagerness to escape at the king's approach. His Majesty, who was on foot, now appeared at the entrance, followed by his pages. He waved his hand and called me to him. Immediately two attendants brought chairs and placed them on the grass opposite to each other. The king offered me one, and then entered into conversation with me, while the whole escort and every one near us remained prostrate on the ground; as far as the eye could reach, not a soul was standing.

'How do you like my city?' asked the king.

'Sire, it is splendid, and presents an appearance such as I have never seen elsewhere.'

'All the palaces and pagodas which you see from here have been built in one year since my return from Siam: in another year all will be finished. Formerly Cambodia was very extensive; but the Annamites have deprived us of many provinces.'

'Sire, the time has arrived for you to retake them. The French are assailing them on one side; do you attack them on the other.' His Majesty did not reply, but offered me a cigar, and inquired my age.

'I am twenty-three,' he said to me. 'I recognise you; you were at Siam with M. de Montigny.'

'No, sire; your Majesty is mistaken. I have only been in Siam a twelvemonth.'

I then sent for an elegant small Minié rifle, which the king's officers had examined in the morning, and presented it to him, asking him if he would deign to accept it. He desired me to load it, which I did. 'It is done, sire,' said I.

'Is it possible? Fire, then.'

He chose for a target a post some way off, and pointed out the place he wished me to hit. I fired, and immediately his Majesty and the pages went to satisfy themselves that the aim was true.

'When do you wish to leave Udong?'

'Sire, I should like to depart, the day after to-morrow, for Pinhalu and the other provinces.'

'If you could remain one day longer, it would give me pleasure. Tomorrow you will dine with me; on the day after I will take you to see the town of the first king, and in the evening we will have a play.'

The play, I thought, will be curious, and therefore I decided to remain; and, after I had thanked the king for his kindness to me, he shook hands with me, and we separated. Evidently I was in high favour. On the following morning messengers came from the king to place horses at my disposal, should I be inclined to ride; but the heat was too great. About four in the afternoon he again did me the honour of sending a horse to bring me to the palace. I wore a white coat, vest, and trousers; a helmet made of cork, after the fashion of the ancient Romans, and covered with white muslin, completed my singular toilet.

I was introduced by the chamberlain into one of the king's private apartments, a pretty room furnished in the European style. His Majesty sat waiting for me, smoking, near a table covered with refreshments; and as soon as I entered he rose, and holding out his hand, and smiling, he begged me to sit down and begin my repast. I perceived that he intended, after the manner of the country, to do me honour by being present at the meal without partaking of it himself.

After introducing me, with much courtesy and friendliness, to his brother, a young man of fifteen, who was kneeling by his side, the king said, 'I have had this fowl and duck cooked in European fashion; tell me if they are to your taste.'

All had been really exceedingly well prepared; the fish, particularly, was capital.

'Good brandy,' said the king, in English (the only words he

knew in that language), as he pointed to a bottle of cognac. 'Drink,' continued he.

The attendants then placed before me jellies and exquisitely preserved fruits, bananas, and excellent mangoes. Afterwards tea was served, of which the king also partook, having first offered me a Manilla cigar. He then wound up a musical-box, and put it on the table. The first air gave me great pleasure, all the more because I was unprepared to hear it in a royal palace. It was the *Marseillaise*. The king took my start and look of astonishment for admiration. 'Do you know that air?' he asked.

'Yes, sire.'

Then followed another scarcely less familiar, the air of the Girondins, *Mourir pour la patrie*.

'Do you also know that?'

As an answer, I accompanied the air with the words. 'Does your Majesty like this air?' I inquired.

'Not so well as the first.'

'Your Majesty is right; most European sovereigns have the same taste.'

'Napoleon, for instance?'

'Napoleon, particularly.'

My Annamite was with me, and filled the office of interpreter, with a perfect tact which pleased the king. The young prince now asked permission to retire, and saluted his brother by bowing to the earth and raising his clasped hands above his head. The king desired him to return the next morning, and accompany us to the palace of the first king; and the prince, passing out into the court-yard, was lifted astride on the shoulders of an attendant, and carried to his palace.

His Majesty then displayed to me his European furniture, mahogany tables covered with china vases and other ornaments of a commonplace description; above all, he pointed out, as worthy of notice, two old-looking glasses in gilt frames, a sofa, and various similar articles. 'I am but beginning,' said he; 'in a few years my palace will be beautiful.'

He afterwards took me into his garden, where were some rare and curious plants, and a miniature artificial rock. Then, on returning to the sitting-room, he conducted me past the inmates of his seraglio, at least a hundred in number, whom curiosity had brought out to gaze at the stranger.

'You are the first foreigner who has ever been admitted here,' he said to me. 'In Cambodia, as in Siam, no one but the people on duty can penetrate into the king's private apartments.'

I thanked him for the honour he had done me, and took leave. He told me to ask for all I wanted, and he would refuse no request. The only thing I desired was to have my journey facilitated; and to this end I begged him to furnish me with letters to the chiefs of the different provinces of his dominions, and one or two elephants. This he promised to do.

The next morning the king sent for me at ten o'clock. I found him seated on a sofa in the reception-hall, giving orders to his pages about the order of march to be observed in going and returning. When all was ready, he entered a sedan-chair or palanquin magnificently carved and painted. His head and feet were bare, his hair cut in the Siamese fashion, and he wore a superb *langouti* of yellow silk, with a girdle of the same material, but of a lighter shade. The palanquin was borne on the shoulders of four attendants, and another held up an enormous red parasol with a gilt handle upwards of twelve feet long. The youngest prince, carrying the king's sabre, walked beside him; I was on the other side, and his Majesty often turned towards me to point out any striking object, and trying to read in my face what I thought of the effect produced on the

people by his appearance. He sat in a careless attitude, one leg
hanging out of the palanquin, and with his elbow resting on the
morocco cushions.

At the approach of the procession all the collected population
bowed themselves to the ground. In front marched three lictors,
bearing in their hands bundles of rattans (the emblems of power);
behind the palanquin came, two and two, the chamberlains and
pages, numbering more than thirty, all dressed in red, and bearing
on their shoulders pikes, sabres, or guns in cases. In this order we
arrived at the outer entrance of the palace of the first king.

His Majesty here descended from his palanquin, and, still in the
same order of march, we proceeded along an avenue about half a
mile in length, planted with young trees, and bounded on either
side by a wooden fence. The ground slopes gradually from hence,
and is laid out in gardens and lawns, encircling which are a hundred
little cottages with walls of clay and thatched roofs. 'All these
houses are inhabited by my father's wives; there is not a man in
them,' said the young king.

Farther on was a lake surrounded with rich and luxuriant verdure. On its banks, buried in foliage, which is reflected in the clear
water, stands the royal residence, part of which is of bamboo, the
rest being white-washed. We went through several apartments, in
which poor Annamite women were weaving silk, and, after passing
in front of the treasury and the king's magazines, finally reached
a vast hall which, here, is peculiarly called the palace. The interior
does not come up to what might be expected from an outside
view. It is stocked like a bazaar with glass bottles, vases filled with
artificial flowers and covered by glass shades, cushions of all colours
and sizes, boxes, slippers, old sofas, looking-glasses, washing-stands,
and a variety of European articles, piled upon tables and shelves,
and on the floor. As the young king was to spend the day at the

palace, he now dismissed me, appointing one of his chamberlains to escort me home.

A little after sunset the people collected in crowds to witness the play which was to be performed on the king's return, expected at seven o'clock. The multitude was so dense that not a single inch of ground in the courtyard was unoccupied, and the walls, even, were all covered. At these festivities the people are apparently permitted to depart from the customary posture of humility, for every one was seated in Oriental fashion. The play was simply a phantasmagoria tolerably well managed, and accompanied by music more noisy than harmonious; but which appeared perfectly to satisfy the public.

V

AMONG THE MISSIONARIES

On the 2nd July, having taken our usual morning repast of rice, we were ready to set off, and were only waiting for the waggons and elephants promised me by the king. They were not long in arriving, and we passed through the city amidst an immense crowd of people who had come from all quarters to witness our departure. We were mounted on our elephants, and escorted by several of the royal pages as far as the road to Pinhalu; all the population prostrating themselves as before the king, doubtless because he had paid me such marked attention.

We proceeded, at the rate of about three miles an hour, on a good road, which was in some places raised more than ten feet above the level of the wooded but marshy plain which extends to the great arm of the Mekon.

Now and then we crossed handsome bridges built of stone or wood, which certainly give a more favourable idea of the state of engineering in Cambodia than in Siam; for, even at Bangkok, the streams and canals are spanned by thin, narrow planks, or by trunks of trees thrown across by the inhabitants, and not by the authorities. We met many pedestrians laden, probably, with provisions for the market. The road is bordered with miserable bamboo huts, like poultry-houses, raised on piles.

We arrived early the same day at Pinhalu, a village of some size, situated on the right bank of the stream, many of the inhabitants of which are the descendants of Portuguese and Annamite refugees. It is the residence of a French bishop, Monsignor Miche, Vicar-apostolic of the mission to Cambodia and Laos. He was absent, but I found three good and benevolent missionaries, who begged me to wait for his return, and received me in that cordial and affectionate manner which is so pleasant to meet with in a strange land, and especially from fellow-countrymen. M. Fontaine, the eldest of the three, though still in the prime of life, had been a missionary for nearly twenty years. He was formerly attached to the mission at Cochin-China, and I had seen him on my visit to Bangkok, where he remained some time before going to Cambodia. He was then feeble and suffering, but I was glad now to find him stronger and full of animation. I felt a true respect for this worthy man; may there be many labourers in the same vocation resembling him!

The second priest, M. Arnoux, was not only a fellow-countryman, but our birthplaces were only distant from each other a few leagues. He was born in the department of Russey, and I in that of Montbéliard (Doubs), so that I had two reasons for being drawn towards him. He belongs to the Cochin-China mission, and had come from among the savage Stiêns to renew his stock of provisions; but, having been attacked by dysentery, owing to the fatigue of the journey, he had been unable to return. These two valiant soldiers of the Church, with good and pure hearts, iron wills, and the energy and courage of heroes, or, rather, of martyrs, had formerly lived together, at a distant station, among the savage Benous, and had suffered there terribly from fevers, dysentery, scurvy, and other diseases. On hearing these brave and worthy sons of our dear country describe their past and present misery, I was sometimes as much amused as affected, with so much liveliness was the narration given; but it is the characteristic of our dauntless nation that her sons suffer and die gaily, and with smiles on their lips.

Four days flew by rapidly in the society of these friends, by whom I was detained till the return of their bishop, whose acquaintance I much desired to make. I knew that I should find in him a man of very superior character; but I did not expect to find in this eminent missionary a simplicity and humility equal to his talents and strength of mind. Monsignor Miche is short and slight; but under his frail exterior exist extraordinary energy and endurance.

I now determined to visit the savage tribes living to the east of the great river, 104° east long. from Paris, and of whom I had heard M. Arnoux speak; he had promised me a welcome from M. Guilloux, the missionary there. I sent Niou back to Udong to ask the king for the letter he had promised. He soon returned with it in due form, and on the 22nd July I quitted Pinhalu, in a small boat with two rowers, which I hired as far as Pemptiélan, situated on the Mekon river, about forty miles to the north of Penom-Penh.

Ever since I had been in Cambodia my servants had been in a state of alarm, and it reached its height when I informed them that we were about to set out on an expedition to the savage tribes. Cambodia is much dreaded by the Siamese: and the mountains, and, still more, the forests, inhabited by the Stiêns, have a reputation for unhealthiness, among both Cambodians and Annamites, equal to that which, in France, is enjoyed by Cayenne, whither condemned political offenders and malefactors from the galleys are sent to die. I doubt very much if I could have met with any other men who would have remained with me.

On descending the great arm of the Mekon, which is here 1200 metres wide, I was astonished at seeing the current running from south to north instead of following the course of the river into which it falls. During more than five months of the year, the great lake of Cambodia, Tonli-Sap, covers an immense space of ground: after that period there is a diminution in depth owing to the great evaporation, but its width remains nearly unaltered. Although its waters increase in volume during the rainy season, these are not swelled by the streams from the mountains on its western boundary, but by the strength of the current from the Mekon which pours into it its overflow.

We left Pinhalu at eleven, and by evening had reached the great bazaar of Cambodia, the distance being about eighteen miles. I had little to buy, for M. Miche and M. Arnoux had insisted on filling my boat with rice and dried fish, sufficient to last not only for my voyage but during the whole period I proposed to remain among the Stiêns.

I stopped a whole day to see the city, and make a few purchases of glass, brass wire, and cotton yarn, articles which would be useful as barter among the savages. The town is situated at the confluence of two great streams, and contains about 10,000 inhabitants, almost all Chinese; but it has a floating population of more than double that number, composed of Cambodians and Cochin-Chinese, living in their boats. It was the time when most of the fishermen, returning from the great lake, stop at Penom-Penh to sell part of their fish, and when a crowd of small merchants flock there to buy cotton, which is gathered in before the rains.

Although the missionaries often pass through Penom-Penh, my presence excited much curiosity among the people. The war in Cochin-China was the subject of all conversations, and in every one's thoughts. The reports of the Chinese and Annamites who had seen the taking of the town of Saigon were not flattering to the pride of a Frenchman.

The next day, descending the river toward the southern extremity of the city, we passed a floating town, composed of more than 500 boats, most of them of large size. They serve as an entrepot for some merchants, and residences for others. All their money and the greater part of their merchandize is here kept, that, in case of alarm, they may be ready to take flight at a moment's warning.

Shortly afterwards we entered the Mekon, which was only now beginning to rise, as, throughout the country the drought had been excessive, lasting much longer than usual. This great river, the name of which signifies 'Mother of Rivers', recalled to my mind the Menam, north of Bangkok, but its aspect is less gay; yet there is something very imposing in this expanse of water running with all the rapidity of a torrent. A few boats, scarcely distinguishable, toiled along: the banks, generally about 18 or 20 feet high, seemed almost deserted; and the forests were indistinctly discernible more than a mile beyond. In Siam the elegant foliage of the bamboos and palm-trees shows out strikingly against the blue sky, while the songs of the birds charm the ear: here, shoals of porpoises sail along with their noses to the wind, frequently bounding out of the water; pelicans sport on the margins of the stream, and herons and storks fly silently from among the reeds at our approach. These are the sole objects of interest.

We passed the great island of Ko-Sutin, which is distant about 40 miles from Penom-Penh, after five days' difficult and laborious travelling. The current of the Mekon is so strong that at certain times of the year you can go little more than a league a day, and the rowers often seek for fire in the evening at the very place where they cooked their rice in the morning. I ascended it in a small boat with three rowers, but at every bend of the river we had the greatest trouble to make any progress, and were frequently obliged to hold on by the rushes to prevent our being carried away by the current.[1]

About 25 or 30 leagues north of Ko-Sutin, on the confines of Laos, commence the rapids and cataracts: it is then necessary to leave the boats and take to pirogues, which, as well as the luggage, have often to be carried on men's backs.

I made a halt of only a few hours, in order to see another voluntary exile, M. Cordier, a priest of great worth, from the Cambodian mission, who resides here. I felt great compassion for this good

[1] In this and following paragraphs I have included some additional material which Mouhot put in a letter for the R.G.S. dated 15 October 1859.

man, on entering the chapel which he had built, and seeing the poverty and nakedness around. He came to meet me, and invited me to share his repast. For the last three years the poor missionary has been suffering from a dysentery, which has become chronic. However, he complains neither of his bad health nor of his poverty: the only thing that grieved him was the small number of converts he was called on to baptize, so deeply are the Cambodians attached to their idols.

'But you,' said he to me; 'do you know whither you are going? I am astonished that they allowed you to leave Pinhalu. Ask the Cambodians what they think of the forests of the Stiêns, and propose to some of them to accompany you: you would not find one. The rains have begun, and you are going to almost certain death, or will at least catch a fever, which will be followed by years of languor and suffering. I have had the jungle fever, and it is something terrible: even to the tips of my nails I felt a heat which I can only call infernal: sometimes an icy coldness would take its place: generally people sink under it: witness M. Lafitte, a young missionary, who a short time ago took the same journey; M. Comte, who died of exhaustion; and many others.'

This account was not reassuring, nevertheless I had determined on my route: I knew that I should find there land and fresh-water shells which I could find nowhere else, and that this tribe of almost unknown savages would afford me a curious and interesting study; and these considerations were sufficient to determine me to proceed. I trusted in God, and went on my way, M. Cordier's last words being, 'May God be with the poor traveller!'

Twelve miles higher up I left the river, and set off on my land journey at two o'clock in the afternoon, hoping to arrive the same day at Pemptiélan, a large village, where lived the mandarin to whom the king's letter was addressed. We did not, however, get there till eleven the next morning, having to pass the night at the foot of a tree, where we lighted a fire. I waited at once upon the mandarin, who is governor of the district, and he received me very well, in spite of the small value of the presents I made him, and immediately gave orders for waggons to be made ready for me. He then presented me with a quantity of tobacco and betel. His manners were, for a Cambodian, gentle and polished; and he questioned me much as to the war in Cochin-China, as well as about Europe, how long it took to get there, &c.

From the time we left Pemptiélan we had, except at rare intervals, to pass through dense forests. The first day our conveyances upset, and I feared that we should be unable to proceed; there were continually dreadful bogs, quagmires, and marshes, in which the carts sank up to the axle-trees and the buffaloes to their bellies. Fortunately on the following day the road improved, but for three weeks all that was visible was a few scattered rice-fields round the villages, and we had to make our way through a marshy plain, covered with thick and dark woods, which reminded one of the enchanted forest of Tasso, and it is easy to understand that the imagination of a pagan race peoples these gloomy solitudes with evil spirits. Twenty times in an hour the men who accompanied us were obliged to raise the large branches and cut down the trunks which obstructed our passage, and sometimes we had to make a new path for ourselves.

We had only been able to accomplish 60 miles in five days, and were still 30 miles from Brelum. I grew tired of the incivility of the inhabitants from whom I hired the oxen, and of the slowness of these animals: when we had no shelter for the night, we suffered much from rain and damp; our clothes were almost always soaked through. The Cambodians were all much surprised at seeing us journeying towards the Stiêns at the worst time of the year, for in that country the rainy season had commenced, and even those who live nearest dare not venture there; and had I not brought with me from Siam my two young servants, I could not for any money have found a single individual to accompany me. Even they felt great repugnance to proceed—for in Siam, Cambodia bears a terrible reputation for unhealthiness, and unhappily both for them and for myself they were attacked with fever—the Annamite particularly, who had a tertian fever, lasting for ten days—since which, instead of receiving any help from them, I have had two patients to nurse.

Passing through a village peopled by a barbarous race of Annamites, I ran great risk of being taken prisoner by them, and being sent to finish my researches in a dungeon. Last year the carriages belonging to a French missionary were completely rifled, and the men sent with ropes round their necks to Cochin-China. I loaded all my guns, and gave one to each of my men: our firm appearance, no doubt, frightened them, for we were not attacked.

The poverty of the inhabitants of these miserable villages engenders a repulsive dirtiness: a strip of matting or an old filthy cushion thrown on the ground, and full of vermin, some basins of coarse Chinese porcelain, a sort of hatchet, and a piece of cotton, intended either for a counterpane, scarf, or cloak, according to the season and time of day, are the usual contents of a Cambodian hut.

In spite of the letter given to me by the King of Cambodia, ordering all the chiefs of the Srok Khmer, or Cambodian villages, to furnish me with the means of transport on my journey, I experienced much difficulty, as frequently neither buffaloes nor carts were to be found in the hamlets through which I passed. My journey took me a month to accomplish, which is about three times as long as it would have taken me on foot.

We arrived at Pump-Ka-Daye, on the confines of Cambodia,

and inhabited by about twenty Stiêns, who have approached the boundary in order to escape slavery in their own tribe. Our waggons halted before a small caravanserai, open to every wind; and after having carried in our luggage, our guides disappeared much faster than they had come. The chief soon presented himself, followed by some men: he had all the characteristics of a savage in his face, and of a Cambodian in his nature. I handed him my letter, but he returned it, saying that he could not read. 'These, then,' said I, 'are the contents. It is the king's order to all chiefs of villages where I shall stop to furnish me with waggons to continue my journey to Brelum.' 'We have no waggons,' was the answer.

We made ourselves as comfortable as we could till the next day, when a second interview with the chief proved to me that I should get no aid from him. I therefore sent Niou with two Cambodians to carry a letter to M. Guilloux, and bring me an answer. This arrived on the evening of the fourth day; and in it M. Guilloux assured me of a cordial welcome, adding that he was interested in my undertaking, and had already a great regard for me, without seeing me, for my courage in coming so far. The good father sent me three waggons from the mission settlement, and some of his Annamites, as well as two Stiêns, to help me on my way. This letter completely removed all fear of being a troublesome and unwelcome guest to the poor hermit, and I set out with pleasure and confidence. It took us two long days' journey to reach Brelum: we encamped one night near a torrent, lying on our mats beside a good fire, which we lighted to keep off the ferocious denizens of these forests. The second night we passed in a deserted cabin some miles from Brelum; and on the 16th August, at nine in the morning, we came to a clearing of from 250 to 300 metres square. We were betwixt two hills, at the foot of which was marshy ground. On the slope of one I saw two long bamboo houses, covered with thatch, and with the mission-garden attached: higher up was the cross planted two years before amidst these frightful solitudes by the noble and courageous French missionaries.

Scarcely had we appeared when we were saluted by a discharge of musketry. We replied as well as we could; and while these sounds were reverberating among the echoes of the forests, poor Father Guilloux, his legs covered with bad wounds, which had confined him for above six months to his mattress, and which he had received on the journeys undertaken through the promptings of his pious zeal, advanced with frail steps to meet me along the tree-trunks thrown as a bridge across the swamp. All honour to thee, noble son of our dear and beautiful country!

VI

THE ABORIGINES
OF CAMBODIA

IN spite of the heat, the fatigue, and privations inseparable from such a journey, I arrived among the Stiêns in perfectly good health as far as I was concerned. It would have been impossible to go further, for I could neither find means of transport nor provisions, for at this time of the year the poor savages have consumed all their rice, and have nothing to live upon but herbs, a little maize, and what they can catch in the chase.

We are surrounded by forests, which are infested with elephants, buffaloes, rhinoceros, tigers, and wild boars, and the ground all about the pools is covered with their footprints. We live almost as in a beseiged place, every moment dreading some attack of the enemy, and keeping our guns constantly loaded. Sometimes they come close to our quarters, and we cannot go even a few steps into the woods without hearing them. As a general rule, however, they fly from the approach of man, and in order to get a shot it is necessary to lie in wait either amongst the branches of a tree or hidden amid the brushwood near the spots where they come to drink.

Scorpions, centipedes, and, above all, serpents, were the enemies we most dreaded, and against which precautions were chiefly requisite; but the mosquitoes and the leeches, though less dangerous, were the most troublesome and most inveterate plagues. During the rainy season you cannot be too much on your guard; going to bed or getting up, you are ever in peril of putting hand or foot on some venomous snake. I have killed more than one in my house with a gun or a hatchet. As I write, I am obliged to be continually on the watch, fearing to see one reappear on which I trod this evening, but which made his exit without hurting me. From time to time, also, I stop to listen to the roaring of a tiger, who is wandering round our dwelling and looking longingly at the pigs through their fence of planks and bamboos. Again, I hear a rhinoceros breaking down the bamboos which oppose his progress towards the brambles encircling our garden, on which he intends to banquet.

If you ask who are this strange people, living retired on the table-lands and mountains of Cambodia, which they appear never to have quitted, and differing entirely in manners, language, and features from the Annamites, Cambodians, and Laotians, my answer is that I believe them to be the aborigines of the country, and that they have been driven into these districts by the repeated inroads of the Thibetians, from whom they evidently descend, as is proved by the resemblance of features, religion, and character.

The whole country from the eastern side of the mountains of Cochin-China as far as 103° long., and from 11° lat. to Laos, is inhabited by savage tribes, all known under one name, which signifies 'inhabitants of the heights'. They have no attachment to the soil, and frequently change their abode; most of the villages are in a state of continual hostility with each other, but they do not attack in troops, but seek to surprise each other, and the prisoners are sold as slaves to the Laotians.

Their only weapon is the cross-bow, which they use with extraordinary skill, but rarely at a distance of more than twenty paces. Poisoned arrows are used only for hunting the larger animals, such as elephants, rhinoceros, buffaloes, and wild oxen, and with these the smallest scratch causes death, if the poison is fresh; the strongest animal does not go more than 50 paces before it falls; they then cut out the wounded part, half roast it without skinning or cutting it up, after which they summon the whole village by sound of trumpet to partake of it. The most perfect equality and fraternity reign in these little communities. The strongest European would find it difficult to bend the bow which the Stiên, weak and frail as he appears, bends without effort, doubtless by long practice.

They are not unacquainted with agriculture, but grow rice and plant gourds, melons, bananas, and other fruit-trees; their rice-fields are kept with the greatest care, but nearly all the hard work is done by the women. They seldom go out in the rainy season on account of the leeches, which abound in the woods to such a degree as to render them almost unapproachable; they remain in their fields, where they construct small huts of bamboo, but as soon as the harvest is over and the dry season returns they are continually out fishing or hunting. They never go out without their baskets on their backs, and carrying their bows and a large knife-blade in a bamboo handle. They forge nearly all their instruments from ore which they procure from Annam and Cambodia. Although they know how to make earthen vessels, they generally cook their rice and herbs in bamboo. Their only clothing is a strip of cloth passed between the thighs and rolled round the waist. The women weave these scarfs, which are long and rather pretty, and which when well made often sell for as much as an ox. They are fond of ornaments, and always have their feet, arms, and fingers covered with rings made of thick brass wire; they wear necklaces of glass beads, and their ears are pierced with an enormous hole, through which they hang the bone of an animal, or a piece of ivory sometimes more than three inches in circumference. They wear their hair long in the Annamite fashion, and knot it up with a comb made of bamboo; some pass through it a kind of arrow made of brass wire, and ornamented by a pheasant's crest.

Their features are handsome and sometimes regular, and many wear thick mustachios and imperials.

Quite alone and independent amidst their forests, they scarcely recognise any authority but that of the chief of the village, whose dignity is generally hereditary. For the last year or two the King of Cambodia has occasionally sent the mandarin who lives nearest the Stiêns to their first villages, in order to distribute marks of honour to their chiefs, hoping little by little to subdue them, and to get from them slaves and ivory, and already he receives a small tribute every year. His emissaries, however, scarcely dare pass the limits of the kingdom, so fearful are they of the arrows of the savages and of the fevers which reign in their forests.

The Stiên is gentle and hospitable, and possesses neither the stupid pride of the Cambodian, nor the refined cruelty and corruption of the Annamite. He is the 'good fellow' of the forest, simple and even generous; his faults are those common to all Asiatics, namely, cunning, an extraordinary power of dissimulation, and idleness; his great passion is hunting, and he leaves work to the women, but, unlike the Cambodians, robbery is very rare among them.

They believe in a supreme being, but only invoke the evil spirit to induce him to leave them in peace. They bury the dead near their dwellings. They do not believe in metempsychosis, but think that animals have also souls which live after their death, and continue to haunt the places they frequented in their lives. Their superstitions are numerous; the cry of an owl, or the sight of a crow, just as they are about to set off on a journey, they consider a bad augury, which is sufficient to turn them from their plans.

When any one is ill they say it is the demon tormenting him, and keep up night and day a frightful uproar round him, which only ceases when one of the bystanders falls as in a fit crying out, 'He has passed into me, he is stifling me.' They then question the new patient as to the remedies which must be employed to cure the sick man, and as to what the demon demands to abandon his prey. Sometimes it is an ox, a pig, too often a human victim; in the latter case they pitilessly seize on some poor slave, and immolate him without remorse.

They imagine that all white people inhabit secluded corners of the earth in the midst of the sea, and often ask if there are any women in our country. When and how I can return to Cambodia and Siam I am ignorant, and I dare not think of the difficulty I shall experience among the rude and stupid Cambodians in transporting my treasures. What heart-breaking jolts my boxes of insects will receive! What palpitations I shall feel each time some rough fellow takes them to place on the oxen, elephants, or his own back! Poor soldiers of science! these are our trophies, and in the eyes of some people find as much merit as a piece of silk fastened to a pole; and what pains, patience, and solicitude is necessary to procure them! therefore I believe my anxiety as to my collections will be understood by the lovers of nature.[1]

Polygamy is held in honour among the Stiêns, although only the chiefs are rich enough to allow themselves the luxury of several wives.

While I was among them there was a total eclipse of the sun, which, if I remember right, was also visible in England. Like the Cambodians, on the occurrence of such phenomena, they believe that some being has swallowed up the sun and moon; and in order to deliver them, they made a frightful noise, beat the tam-tam, uttered savage cries, and shot arrows into the air, until the sun re-appeared.

One of their favourite amusements is to send up kites, to which they attach a musical instrument somewhat resembling a bow, and this, when agitated by the wind, produces sweet and melodious sounds to which they are fond of listening.

The Fauna of this country does not differ much from that of the kingdom of Siam; thus, with the exception of some beautiful new species of insects and land shells, and a number of interesting birds,

---

[1] The additional material which I have added from Mouhot's letter of 15th October 1859 ceases at this point.

I shall gain by my excursion nothing but the pleasure of having been able to study the habits of a curious people, and the not inferior gratification of making them known to the public, should these rough notes, written hastily, and with no claim to any merit but truth, be destined to see the light. Whether God reserves for me the happiness of again seeing my native country, in which event it will be my endeavour to put them into some sort of readable shape; or whether I fall a victim to pestilence or ferocious beasts, and some kind person takes charge of these sheets, scribbled generally by the light of a torch, and on my knees at the foot of a tree, amidst interruptions of all sorts, of which the mosquitoes are not the least annoying; in either case, living or dead, I shall need, I am aware, an indulgence seldom granted. Most readers prefer being amused to being instructed; while my sole aim has been to paint faithfully, and to the best of my poor abilities, what came under my observation.

My arrival here was—I may say it without vanity, for I was a stranger to him—quite an event in the poor missionary's lonely life; and the landing—for it did not deserve the name of room— left vacant by the departure of Father Arnoux, was placed at my disposal. I ask pardon of the good, brave, and generous priests who have aided, welcomed, and sheltered me through all my wanderings, if I have spoken too plainly of their poverty and privations of all kinds; if I have raised the curtain which, perhaps, they would wish to keep drawn, for, I repeat, they look not for recompense in this world; but I have done it that the world may know that their life is one of the hardest and most painful, and requires self-sacrifice more than any other. Exposed to the influence of pernicious climates, badly lodged, badly fed, far from their families and from their country, often ill and dying without help—such is the lot of these men.

The house of uncle Apait was at least as elegant and well furnished as that of the humble priest of Brelum: both had the bare ground for a floor, walls of bamboo canes, and dried grass for thatch. The hut was divided into four compartments, two being used by the missionaries, another by their servant, and the fourth served as a chapel. This, like the others, was far from splendid, and the whole house had been so undermined by the white ants, that it seemed menaced with approaching ruin.

During the three months I passed in Brelum and its environs, my two poor servants were almost constantly ill with fever. I think myself very fortunate to have preserved my health, for even in these forests I have not had a touch of this complaint. In the rainy season the atmosphere is dreadfully damp and oppressive; in the thickest wood, where the sun scarcely penetrates, you might fancy yourself in a stove, and with the slightest exercise you are in a bath of perspiration.

In July and August we experienced violent storms, which burst out every second or third day; but in September and October it rained without intermission. At the beginning of November, after a change of wind, we had some refreshing nights, which made the thermometer fall to 12° centigrade. From noon to three o'clock there was little variation in the temperature.

Having paid visits to all the villages in the neighbourhood, and been visited in return by many of the inhabitants, I announced to my two excellent friends the missionaries that I must shortly leave them, and fixed my departure for the 29th November, meaning to return to Pinhalu and Udong, and from thence to ascend the Mekon as far as the great lake Tonli-Sap.

On the 29th I took my leave of my amiable fellow-countryman and friend, M. Arnoux,[1] to, I may venture to affirm, our mutual

[1] Father Arnoux had arrived back at Brelum during Mouhot's stay.

regret, and set off, accompanied by Father Guilloux, who had some business at Pinhalu. The rains had ceased for the last three weeks, and I was agreeably surprised at the improvement in the state of the country since August. The paths were dry, and we had no longer to flounder through dirty marshes, nor suffer from the wet nights which we formerly found so unpleasant. When we reached the station where we were to pass the first night, our servants lighted a fire to cook their rice, as well as scare away the wild beasts; but, notwithstanding this, we remarked that our oxen, dogs, and monkey showed signs of great fear, and, almost immediately afterwards, we heard a roaring like that of a lion. We seized our guns, which were loaded, and waited in readiness.

Fresh roarings, proceeding from a very short distance off, completed the terror of our animals; and we ourselves could not help feeling uneasy. I proposed to go and meet the enemy, which was agreed to, and we accordingly plunged into that part of the forest whence the sound came. Although familiar with these terrible creatures, we felt far from comfortable; but before long we came upon recent tracks which were quite unmistakeable, and soon, in a small clearing in the forest, perceived nine elephants, the leader being a male of enormous size, standing right in front of us.

On our approach he set up a roar more frightful than ever, and the whole herd advanced slowly towards us. We remained in a stooping position, half hidden behind the trees, which were too tall for us to climb. I was in the act of taking aim at the forehead of the leader, the only vulnerable part, but an Annamite who stood beside me, and who was an old hunter, knocked up my rifle, and begged me not to fire; 'for,' said he, 'if you kill or wound one of the elephants we are lost; and even if we should succeed in escaping, the oxen, the waggons, and all their contents would be overwhelmed by the fury of these animals. If there were but two or three, we might hope to kill them; but nine, of whom five are very large, are too many; and it will be more prudent to retreat.' At this moment, Father Guilloux, who had not much confidence in his powers of locomotion, fired his gun in the air to frighten the elephants; and this plan fortunately succeeded: the herd stopped in astonishment for an instant, then turned round, and marched into the forest.

When we reached Pemptiélan we stopped at the house of the mandarin, whose authority extends over the neighbouring district, and, contrary to the usual custom, he offered us hospitality under his own roof. Scarcely, however, were we installed when he came to me and asked for the best of my guns, and, on my declining to part with it, he begged for something else, intimating that we should have begun by offering a present. Thereupon I gave him a suit of European clothes, a powder-flask and some powder, a hunting-knife, and some other small articles. In return he presented me with an ivory trumpet, and placed at my service two elephants to enable me to continue my route more comfortably: he likewise sent off our people with a letter to the chiefs of the Srok Khmer.

We resumed our journey on the following day, the Abbé on one elephant, reading his breviary, and I upon another, both of us greatly enjoying the beauty of the landscape. In passing opposite the island of Ko-Sutin we stopped to see Father Cordier. The good missionary was in a sad state: his malady had got worse; and his debility was such that he could scarcely drag himself from his bed to a chair. He had no food but rice and dried fish; and the only persons to care for him, and wait upon him, were two children of ten years old. We begged him to accompany us to Pinhalu, but he declined, on account of his weakness. 'All I regret,' said he, 'is, that I shall see my poor parents no more; but for that, I should await death calmly, and almost with joy.' All our solicitations that he would go with us were unavailing; and we were forced to pursue our journey, very sad at leaving him in so painful a position, and at our inability to give him any relief.

On the 21st December we at last reached Pinhalu.

Ruines de la province
d'Ongcor
Ongcor Wltt.

1er Cahier

Dédié à J. Arrow Smith.
hommage de gratitude & d'affection de la
part de l'auteur

I Above: DAGUERREOTYPE OF HENRI MOUHOT
Below: TITLE PAGE OF MOUHOT'S Cahier

Observations
sur le temple d'ongcor &
sur quelques unes des ruines des provinces
d'Ongor & de Battambong.

Nokhor ou Ongcor était la capitale de l'ancien
royaume du Camboge, si fameux autrefois parmi les
grands états de l'Indo Chine que les seules traditions
qui restent dans le pays, rapportent qu'il comptait
120 roys tributaires, une armée de 5 à 6 millions de sol=
ats, & que les bâtimens du trésor royal occupaient un
space de plus de cent lieues.

Dans la province qui a conservé le même nom &
qui est située à l'Est du grand lac ou Tonli Sap,
comme on l'appelle dans le pays, vers le 14.e degré
de latitude & le 104.me de longitude orientale, méri=
dien de Greenwich, de même aussi, quoique en
moins grand nombre, que dans les provinces de Stoung
& Battambong, sur les bords du Mékon à quelque
distance de Kosutine, & jusque dans l'ancien royaume
Tsiampois, (cochinchine) se trouvent des ruines si im=
posantes, fruits d'un travail tellement éclairé & prodi=
gieux, qu'à leur aspect on se sent saisi de la
plus profonde admiration & que l'on ne cesse de se
demander, l'esprit vivement frappé, ce qu'est devenu
ce peuple puissant, supérieurement civilisé &
éclairé, usquel on pourrait attribuer ces œuvres gigantesques.
un de ces temples surtout œuvres de celui de Salomon, élevé
par d'autres Michel Ange, qui figureraient avec
honneur à côté de nos plus belles basiliques & qui l'em=
portent pour le grandiose sur tout ce que l'art des
grecs ou des romains a jamais édifié, fait un contraste

Mont Ba-Kheng.

Un temple a été élevé au haut d'un mont Ba-Kheng, de sa base, composé de roches calcaires, qui peut avoir quatre vingts à cent mètres de hauteur, & qui se trouve à près de deux milles & demi au nord de Ongcor Wat, sur le chemin même qui conduit à la ville.

Au pied du mont, tout ce que l'on remarque, sont, au milieu des arbres, deux magnifiques lions de — 2 mèt, 20 de haut ne formant qu'un bloc avec les piédestaux qui ont 1,m 80 de long sur 0, 90 de large.

Des escaliers en partie détruits conduisent au sommet du mont, d'où l'on jouit d'une vue si étendue & si belle, que l'on n'est pas étonné que ce peuple de goût ne l'ait couronné en premier lieu d'un splendide monument. D'un côté, l'œil, après avoir plongé sur la plaine boisée & contemple le pyramidal temple d'ongcor & sa riche colonnade, autour desquels ondule le feuillage des cocotiers & des palmiers, va se perdre à l'horizon sur les eaux du grand lac, après s'être arrêté encore un moment sur une nouvelle ceinture de forêts & sur ? petit mont dénudé nommé Crôme qui est au delà de la nouvelle ville.

Du côté opposé, se déroule la longue chaîne de montagnes qui a fourni, dit-on, les riches carrières d'où l'on a extrait tant de beaux blocs de grès, puis, un peu plus à l'ouest & toujours au milieu d'épaisses forêts qui en dérobent une partie,

III PAGE FROM MOUHOT'S DIARY DESCRIBING PHNOM BAKHENG

IV   MONKEYS PLAY WITH A CROCODILE AT CHANTABOUN

V   A BUDDIST MONK IN HIS BOAT

VI   ANGKOR WAT—DETAIL

VII   AN ANCIENT KHMER TOWER

Façade septentrionale des ruines d'Ongkor-Wat.

VIII MOUHOT'S DRAWING OF ANGKOR WAT AS IT WAS WHEN HE REDISCOVERED ANGKOR IN 1860.

IX FAÇADE OF THE TEMPLE OF ONGCOR-WAT.

Drawn by M. Guiaud, from a Sketch by M. Mouhot.

X   CENTRAL PORTICO OF THE GREAT TEMPLE OF ONGCOR-WAT.

Drawn by M. Thérond, from a Sketch by M. Mouhot.

XI   CARAVAN OF ELEPHANTS CROSSING THE MOUNTAINS OF LÁOS.

Drawn by M. Janet Lange, from a Sketch by M. Mouhot

XII · RECEPTION OF M. MOUHOT BY THE KINGS OF LAOS

VII

ANGKOR WAT

I arrived last evening at Pinhalu, in perfect health, and am now about to go northward to visit the famous ruins of Ongcor and then return to Bangkok, so I have little time to give you any details as to what I dispatch from Komput and Singapore. I am not quite satisfied; for birds are scarce here, and I have but a small number; besides, my boxes as I feared have been much knocked about; I sent them off to Komput on men's backs. On my return to Bangkok I will send you some good maps of this almost unknown country.[1]

The entrance to the great lake of Cambodia is grand and beautiful. The river becomes wider and wider, until at last it is four or five miles in breadth; and then you enter the immense sheet of water called Tonli-Sap, as large and full of motion as a sea. It is more than 120 miles long, and must be at least 400 in circumference.

The shore is low, and thickly covered with trees, which are half submerged; and in the distance is visible an extensive range of mountains whose highest peaks seem lost in the clouds. The waves glitter in the broad sunshine with a brilliancy which the eye can scarcely support, and, in many parts of the lake, nothing is visible all around but water. In the centre is planted a tall mast, indicating the boundary between the kingdoms of Siam and Cambodia.

Ere I proceed with my description [of Angkor], I must express my gratitude to the excellent missionary of Battambong, the Abbé E. Silvestre, who, with exceeding courtesy and indefatigable energy, accompanied me through the thick forest which covers a portion of the site of the original building, and by whose assistance I was enabled to accomplish so much in a limited time.

Nokhor, or Ongcor, was the capital of the ancient kingdom of

[1] This paragraph is drawn from the postscript which Mouhot added to his letter written at Brelum and which he carried to Pinhalu himself.

Cambodia, or Khmer, formerly so famous among the great states of Indo-China, that almost the only tradition preserved in the country mentions that empire as having had twenty kings who paid tribute to it, as having kept up an army of five or six million soldiers, and that the buildings of the royal treasury occupied a space of more than 300 miles.

In the province still bearing the name of Ongcor, which is situated east-ward of the great lake Tonli-Sap, towards the 14th degree of north lat., and 104° long. east of Greenwich, there are on the banks of the Mekon, and in the ancient kingdom of Tsiampois (Cochin-China), ruins of such grandeur, remains of structures which must have been raised at such an immense cost of labour, that, at the first view, one is filled with profound admiration, and cannot but ask what has become of this powerful race, so civilised, so enlightened, the authors of these gigantic works?

One of these temples—a rival to that of Solomon, and erected by some ancient Michael Angelo—might take an honourable place beside our most beautiful buildings. It is grander than anything left to us by Greece or Rome, and presents a sad contrast to the state of barbarism in which the nation is now plunged.

Unluckily the scourge of war, aided by time, the great destroyer, who respects nothing, and perhaps also by earthquakes, has fallen heavily on the greater part of the other monuments; and the work of destruction and decay continues among those which still remain standing, imposing and majestic, amidst the masses of ruins all around.

One seeks in vain for any historical souvenirs of the many kings who must have succeeded one another on the throne of the powerful empire of Maha-Nocor-Khmer. There exists a tradition of a leprous king, to whom is attributed the commencement of the great temple, but all else is totally forgotten. The inscriptions, with which some of the columns are covered, are illegible; and, if you interrogate the Cambodians as to the founders of Ongcor-Wat, you invariably receive one of these four replies: 'It is the work of Pra-Eun, the king of the angels'; 'It is the work of the giants'; 'It was built by the leprous king'; or else, 'It made itself.'

The work of giants! The expression would be very just, if used figuratively, in speaking of these prodigious works, of which no one who has not seen them can form any adequate idea; and in the construction of which patience, strength, and genius appear to have done their utmost in order to leave to future generations proofs of their power and civilisation.

It is remarkable that none of these monuments were intended for habitations; all were temples of Buddhism. The statues and bas-reliefs, however, curiously enough, represent entirely secular subjects—monarchs surrounded by their wives, their heads and arms loaded with ornaments such as bracelets and necklaces, the body being covered with a narrow *langouti*. On a sort of esplanade is a statue, said to be that of the leprous king. It is a little above the middle height, and the prince is seated in a noble and dignified attitude. The head, particularly, is a *chef d'œuvre*, the features perfectly regular, and possessing a manly beauty of a description seen now in very rare instances, and only amongst Cambodians of un-mixed race, living in seclusion at the foot of the mountains, where the unhealthiness of the climate condemns them to a solitary existence; or among the savage mountaineers who occupy the border country separating Siam and Cambodia from the kingdom of Annam.

This place was probably chosen for the capital on account of its central position. It is situated fifteen miles from the great lake, in an arid and sandy plain, although the banks of the river would appear to have been a preferable site, more fertile, and offering greater facilities for communication.

Although making no pretension whatever either to architectural or archaeological acquirements, I will endeavour to describe what I saw, for the benefit of others interested in these sciences, and, as well as I can, to draw the attention of Eastern *savants* to a new scene. I shall commence with the temple of Ongcor, the most beautiful and best preserved of all the remains, and which is also the first which presents itself to the eye of the traveller, making him forget all the fatigues of the journey, filling him with admiration and delight, such as would be experienced on finding a verdant oasis in the sandy desert. Suddenly, and as if by enchantment, he seems to be transported from barbarism to civilisation, from profound darkness to light.

Before arriving at Ongcor from Battambong, having previously crossed the great lake from the mouth of either of the currents which traverse both these localities, you come upon a stream, which, in the dry season, you ascend for a couple of miles, and reach a spot where it becomes somewhat larger, forming a small natural basin, which serves the purpose of a kind of harbour. From this place a raised causeway, still passable at the present day, and extending as far as the limit which the waters attain at the period of the inundations, that is to say, over a space of three miles, leads to an insignificant little town, the capital of the province, and situated fifteen miles to the N.N.W. of the shores of the lake.

If, starting from this point, you follow for about a couple of hours in the same direction a dusty sandy path passing through a dense forest of stunted trees; and having also frequently crossed the river, which is exceedingly sinuous in its course, you will arrive at an esplanade about 9 metres wide by 27 long, parallel to the building. At each angle, at the extremity of the two longer sides, are two enormous lions, sculptured out of the rock, and forming, with the pedestals, only a single block. Four large flights of steps lead to the platform.

From the north staircase, which faces the principal entrance, you skirt, in order to reach the latter, a causeway 230 metres in length by 9 in width, covered or paved with large slabs of stone, and supported by walls of great thickness. This causeway crosses a ditch 220 metres wide, which surrounds the building; the revetment, 3 metres high by 1 metre thick, is formed of ferruginous stone, with the exception of the top row, which is of freestone, each block being of the same thickness as the wall.

Principal Entrance. The edifice forms a long gallery with a central tower, and two others, of rather less altitude, about 30 metres distant from the former. The portico of each tower is formed of four projecting columns, with a staircase. At each extremity are similar porticoes, beyond which, but immediately contiguous thereto, is a high door or gateway, on the same level, which serves for the passage of vehicles. From constant use the wheels have worn two deep ruts in the massive flagstones with which the ground is paved.

Upon the west side the gallery is supported by two rows of square columns; on the east, blank windows have been let into the wall, with stone railings or balconies of twisted columns 14 centimetres in diametre. The whole of this side, within one metre of the ground, and half a metre of the cornice, is covered with sculptures executed with marvellously artistic skill.

The roof—and in this respect it resembles all the other buildings —is a double one, constructed externally of sculptured stone, the blocks in the interior being plain; they were formerly hidden by a ceiling, also sculptured, of which some remains may still be remarked. The edifice divides the wall into two equal parts; upon the other sides, and facing the monument, are three pavilions, 33 metres in length.

This imposing colonnade, which, from its great length and beautiful proportions, attracts the attention from a distance, forms a fitting entrance to the great monument.

The Temple. Commencing from the building which forms the principal entrance, is a second causeway, 9 metres wide by 342 metres in length; it is raised 1 metre from the level of the ground. It is covered with huge blocks of stone, carefully joined together throughout its entire length, and is surrounded by a balustrade, partially in ruins, about 1 metre 10 centimetres high, composed of long stones, with bevelled edges, very massive, and covered with sculptures. On each side are six platforms of earth, ascended by several steps, upon each of which is a serpent with seven heads, some erect, others thrown back.

In the centre of the causeway are two elegant pavilions, one on each side, having at each extremity a portico 33 metres 66 centimetres in length. At the end of the causeway, and at the foot of the terrace, are, on each side of the latter, two ponds or sheets of water. A balustrade, like that of the causeway, and resting like it upon a sculptured basement, springs from the foot of the terrace, and runs all round the monument. At certain intervals there are large staircases of several steps each.

The Terrace. The terrace is 2 metres 30 centimetres in height, and is surrounded by 112 fluted columns, surmounted by capitals, formed in each case of one single block of stone. The basement, like that of the whole building, is ornamented with very beautiful sculptured cornices, varied in style, and entirely covered with delicate carvings representing roses and arabesques, worked with the chisel, with a taste and skill equally wonderful.

This terrace forms a cross, each arm of which is 122 metres in

86

length, and 12 metres 16 centimetres wide. There are three flights of steps, upon each of which are four lions reclining upon their pedestals.

The Portico. This is 6 metres in length, and is supported by six columns, four of which are detached from the monument.

The temple is formed of three distinct parts raised in the form of terraces one above the other.

The Galleries. The galleries form a rectangle, the façade of which is 180 metres in length; the sides 216 metres 16 centimetres by 4 metres 16 centimetres.

The vaulted ceilings of the galleries are raised 6 metres from the ground; those of the second roof are 4 metres 30 centimetres high. The two roofs are supported by a double row of columns, the first being 3 metres 18 centimetres and the second 2 metres 25 centimetres high by 48 centimetres broad. The columns are square, and, like all others buildings in the province, are formed of single blocks.

There are five staircases on the west side, the same number on the east, and three on each of the remaining sides.

The basement is 3 metres 90 centimetres in height, the length externally forming a terrace of 1 metre 57 centimetres.

Each portico is composed of three roofs raised one above the other, which contribute materially to give to the architecture of these long galleries a monumental appearance, producing a singularly beautiful effect.

The opposite side of the wall to the double colonnade is, from the lowest row of cornices to one metre above its base, covered inside with bas-reliefs, having externally blank windows with balustrades.

There are two rows of cornices, the first part immediately above the columns; and the space, to the extent of nearly one metre, which lies between them, is filled up by roses and other sculptured designs.

The bas-reliefs represent the combat of the king of the apes with the king of the angels: in the centre is the king of the angels, drawn by two griffins; he has seven heads and twenty arms, with a sabre in each hand. Some of the chiefs are seated in cars drawn by fabulous animals, while others are mounted on elephants. The soldiers are armed with bows, javelins, or sabres, but the apes have generally no weapons except their formidable claws: a few of them have clubs, sabres, or branches of trees.

Peristyle No. 1. Here is represented the march of warriors mounted on birds, horses, tigers, and fabulous animals; the horses of the chiefs are led by the bridle. On the right the soldiers are advancing towards the scene of combat in the centre; but here there are no fantastic animals.

Peristyle No. 2. The bas-reliefs of this peristyle represent the combat between the king of the apes and the king of the angels, and the death of the former. Close by is a boat filled with rowers, all with long beards, and some of them attired in the Chinese fashion: the group is admirable for the natural positions and for the expression given to the faces. A cock-fight, and women at play with their children, are also represented. It is in these bas-reliefs that the highest degree of skill is shown. Other subjects follow, the meaning of which I could not discover.

On the south side, to the left hand, is a military procession—bodies of soldiers headed by chiefs, some mounted on elephants, others on horseback, and each corps carrying different arms, lances, halberds, javelins, sabres, and bows. On the right are two series, one representing the Hindu Paradise Swarga, the other the Hindu infernal regions Naralma. A crowd of persons are entering Paradise, and are received in palanquins: they have with them banners, fans, parasols, and boxes for holding betel, without which even Paradise would not be perfect happiness to a Cambodian.

A triumphal march. Paradise. The elect seated on a magnificent dais, surrounded by a great number of women, with caskets and fans in their hands, while the men are holding flowers and have children on their knees. These appear to be all the joys of Paradise.

The punishments of the infernal regions, on the contrary, are varied and numerous; and while the elect, who are enjoying themselves in Paradise, are all fat and plump, the poor condemned beings are so lean that their bones show through their skin, and the expression of their faces is pitiful and full of a most comic seriousness. Some are being pounded in mortars, while others hold them by the feet and hands; some are being sawn asunder; others are led along, like buffaloes, with ropes through their noses. In other places the *comphubal* (executioners) are cutting men to pieces with sabres; while a crowd of poor wretches are being transfixed by the tusks of elephants, or on the horns of rhinoceros. Fabulous animals are busy devouring some; others are in irons, and have had their eyes put out.

In the centre sits the judge with his ministers, all sabre in hand, and the guilty are dragged before them by the hair or feet. In the distance is visible a furnace and another crowd of people under punishment, being tortured in divers ways—impaled, roasted on spits, tied to trees and pierced with arrows, suspended with heavy weights attached to their hands and feet, devoured by dogs or vultures, or crucified with nails through their bodies.

These bas-reliefs are perfect; the rest are inferior in workmanship and expression.

On the east side, a number of men, divided into two equal groups, are represented as attempting to drag in contrary directions the great serpent or dragon with seven heads, while, in the centre, an angel stands looking on. Many angels are seen floating in the sky above, while fishes, aquatic animals, and marine monsters swim about in a sea visible beneath. The angel is seated on the celebrated mountain of Thibet, Pra Soumer, and in different places angels with several heads give assistance to those pulling the serpent. The king of the apes, Sdach Soa, appears also here.

To the right is a military procession and a combat, the chiefs being mounted on elephants, unicorns, griffins, eagles with peacock's tails, and other fantastic animals, while winged dragons draw the cars.

On the northern side is portrayed a combat, and procession, with drums, flutes, trumpets, tam-tams, and organs said to be Chinese; a king, mounted on the shoulders of a hideous giant, who holds in each hand by the foot a fighting giant. All the chiefs take part in the combat, standing, some on tigers, others in cars.

Near the central peristyle is a figure of the king, with a long beard; on each side are courtiers with clasped hands.

To the right appears a military procession, a combat, griffins, eagles with peacock's tails, a dragon with seven heads and a tower on his back—the king letting fly an arrow, standing on the back of a giant with tail, claws, and beak.

Second Story. The first gallery on the west side is connected with the second by two other smaller galleries, 40 metres long, and which are themselves connected by two colonnades in the form of a cross, and supporting two vaulted roofs.

Four rows of square columns, each hewn out of a single block of stone, those in the inside row being 4 metres 14 centimetres high and 45 centimetres thick; those on the outside being 3 metres 10 centimetres high, and rather smaller at the top than at the base. The little gallery on the right is filled with statues representing persons in the act of worshipping idols, some of these being of wood, others of stone. Many of the statues are 4 metres in height, and the greater number of them must be of great age, to judge from their state of dilapidation, in spite of the hardness of the stone. In the centre is a statue of the famous leprous king, and by his side, in a posture of adoration, are two statues of priests, with faces full of expression. These are real *chefs-d'œuvre*. At no great distance is a small statue of his queen.

Here are found two pavilions of extremely elegant architecture, with porticoes and staircases at each end.

There is a second gallery, with four towers at each end and three porticoes and staircases on each side. This gallery is raised on a base 5 metres 10 centimetres high, the ledge of which forms a terrace 74 centimetres broad.

There are neither columns nor bas-reliefs here, but the walls have imitation windows with twisted bars; the gallery is half dark, receiving very little light except through the doors. There are idols, both of stone and bronze, on pedestals, with their hands held out to receive gifts from their worshippers.

Central part. A raised terrace leads to the foot of the great staircase, and forms a cross, the arms of which lead to two small pavilions with four porticoes and staircases. The base of this part is admirably executed, both as to general effect and in detail. There are twelve staircases, the four in the middle being 6 metres wide, and having 39 steps.

The building forms a square, each side of which is 56 metres 60 centimetres, and at each angle is a tower. A central tower, larger and higher, is connected with the lateral galleries by colonnades covered, like the galleries, with a double roof; and both galleries and colonnades are supported on a base one metre from the floor of the interior courts.

Opposite each of the twelve staircases is a small portico with four columns, 4 metres 50 centimetres high, and 47 centimetres in diameter. Windows, similar in form and dimension to those of the other galleries, are on each side, and have twisted bars carved in stone.

In front of each colonnade, with an entrance in the tower, is a dark and narrow chapel, to which there is an ascent of eight steps. These four chapels do not communicate with each other. Each contains an idol 4 metres in height, sculptured in the solid wall, at whose feet is another nearly 2 metres long, representing Samana-kodom sleeping. The central tower is 33 metres high from the pavement of the gallery, and 50 from the basement of the building.

What strikes the observer with not less admiration than the grandeur, regularity, and beauty of these majestic buildings, is the immense size and prodigious number of the blocks of stone of which they are constructed. In this temple alone are as many as 1532 columns. What means of transport, what a multitude of workmen, must this have required, seeing that the mountain out of which the stone was hewn is thirty miles distant! In each block are to be seen holes $2\frac{1}{2}$ centimetres in diameter and 3 in depth, the number varying with the size of the blocks; but the columns and the sculptured portions of the building bear no traces of them. According to a Cambodian legend, these are the prints of the fingers of a giant, who, after kneading an enormous quantity of clay, had cut it into blocks and carved it, turning it into a hard and, at the same time, light stone by pouring over it some marvellous liquid.

All the mouldings, sculptures, and bas-reliefs appear to have been executed after the erection of the building. The stones are everywhere fitted together in so perfect a manner that you can scarcely see where are the joinings; there is neither sign of mortar nor mark of the chisel, the surface being as polished as marble. Was this incomparable edifice the work of a single genius, who conceived the idea, and watched over the execution of it? One is tempted to think so; for no part of it is deficient, faulty, or inconsistent. To what epoch does it owe its origin? As before remarked, neither tradition nor written inscription furnish any certain information upon this point; or rather, I should say, these latter are as a sealed book for want of an interpreter; and they may, perchance, throw light on the subject when some European *savant* shall succeed in deciphering them.

VIII

ANGKOR THOM

A temple, about 100 metres in height, built of limestone, has been erected on the top of Mount Bakheng, which is situated two miles and a half north of Ongcor-Wat, on the road leading to the town. At the foot of the mountain are to be seen, among the trees, two magnificent lions, one metre 20 centimetres in height, and each formed, with the pedestals, out of a single block. Steps, partly destroyed, lead to the top of the mountain, whence is to be enjoyed a view so beautiful and extensive, that it is not surprising that these people, who have shown so much taste in their buildings, should have chosen it for a site.

On the one side you gaze upon the wooded plain and the pyramidal temple of Ongcor, with its rich colonnades, the mountain of Crome, which is beyond the new city, the view losing itself in the waters of the great lake on the horizon. On the opposite side stretches the long chain of mountains whose quarries, they say, furnished the beautiful stone used for the temples; and amidst thick forests, which extend along the base, is a pretty, small lake, which looks like a blue ribbon on a carpet of verdure. All this region is now as lonely and deserted as formerly it must have been full of life and cheerfulness; and the howling of wild animals, and the cries of a few birds, alone disturb the solitude.

Sad fragility of human things! How many centuries and thousands of generations have passed away, of which history, probably, will never tell us anything: what riches and treasures of art will remain for ever buried beneath these ruins; how many distinguished men—artists, sovereigns, and warriors—whose names were worthy of immortality, are now forgotten, laid to rest under the thick dust which covers these tombs!

The whole summit of the mountain is covered with a coating

of lime, forming a vast smooth surface. At regular intervals are four rows of deep holes, in some of which still stand the columns that formerly supported two roofs, and formed a gallery leading from the staircase to the principal part of the building, and the transverse branches of which were connected with four towers, built partly of stone, partly of brick. Judging from the details of the work, and the state of the stone, which in many places crumbles at a touch, this building belongs to a period much anterior to that of many of the other monuments. Art, like science, was then in its infancy; difficulties were surmounted, but not without great efforts of labour and intelligence; taste was of a grand description, but genius was not in proportion; in a word, the temple of Mount Bakheng appears to have been the prelude to civilisation, while that of Ongcor-Wat was probably its climax.

In the two towers, which are least dilapidated, and which the modern worshippers have covered with a thatched roof, the old one having fallen in, are large idols rudely fashioned, and bearing marks of great age. In one of the other towers is a large stone, the inscription on which is still visible; and on the exterior wall is carved the figure of a king with a long beard, the only portion of bas-relief remaining.

A wall surrounds the top of the mountain. Bakheng has also its Phrabat, but it is a facsimile of recent origin. The building is quadrangular, and composed of five stories, each 3 metres high. That at the base is 68 metres square. They form so many terraces, which serve as bases to seventy-two small but elegant pavilions; and they are enriched with mouldings, colonnades, and cornices, but no sculpture. The work is perfect; and from its good state of preservation would seem to be of a more recent date than the towers. It is evident that each of these little pavilions formerly contained an idol.

Each side of the square has a staircase 2 metres wide, with nine steps to each story, and lions on each terrace. The centre of the terrace formed by the last story is only a confused mass of ruins from the fallen towers. Near the staircase are two gigantic blocks of very fine stone, as polished as marble, and shaped like pedestals for statues.

Half-a-mile beyond Bakheng are the ruins of Ongcor-Thom. A partly-destroyed road, hidden by thick layers of sand and dust, and crossing a large ditch, half filled with blocks of stone, portions of columns, and fragments of sculptured lions and elephants, leads to the gateway of the town, which is built in the style of a triumphal arch.

These remains are in a tolerable state of preservation, and are composed of a central tower, 18 metres high, surrounded by four turrets, and flanked by two other towers connected together by galleries. At the top are four immense heads in the Egyptian style; and every available space is filled with sculpture. At the foot of the great tower is a passage for carriages; and on each side of it are doors and staircases communicating with the walls, the whole building being constructed of sandstone. The outer wall is composed of blocks of ferruginous stone, and extends right and left from the entrance. It is about 24 miles square, 3 met. 80 centimet. thick, and 7 met. high, and serves as a support to a glacis which rises almost from the top. At the four cardinal points are doors, there being two on the east side. Within this vast enclosure, now covered with an almost impenetrable forest, are a vast number of buildings, more or less in ruin, which testify to the ancient splendour of the town. In some places, where the heavy rains have washed away the soil, or where the natives have dug in search for treasure, may be seen immense quantities of porcelain and pottery.

Within the enclosure of Ongcor Thom, and two miles from the

west gate, are to be seen through the trees the tops of the high towers of a building called by the Cambodians 'Prea sat Ling poun', that is to say, 'The Pagoda where they play hide and seek'.[1] It is a collection of 37 towers of unequal size, connected by galleries which cross each other perpetually, and form a labyrinth through which it is not easy to find one's way. A long shallow ditch, crossed by four roads leading to the principal entrances, surrounds it on all sides. Beyond the ditch rises the wall of a gallery, of which the exterior colonnades and the roof are only a mass of ruins, over which you must climb to reach the interior. This wall is still intact: it is about 120 metres long, and forms a square round the pagoda. About 1 metre from the ground are visible, in places where the blocks fallen from the roof have not hidden everything, various bas-reliefs carved in the thickness of the wall: they are not sur-mounted by cornices as at Ongcor-Wat, by which it would seem as if they had never been finished.

Besides the four principal entrances there were other doors at unequal distances in this gallery, but singularly enough many of them have been walled up. The gallery was connected with the main body of the building by four smaller ones opposite each of the great doors, and forming a covered way to the interior; but all these galleries are destroyed.

The second enclosure is 65 metres square, and each front is com-posed of five towers, connected by galleries. The central and corner towers are the largest: they are about 13 metres high. High galleries connect the centre tower with the intermediate ones, which again are connected with those at the corners by galleries of a less elevation.

On each side are seven staircases, of six steps each, and leading either to towers or galleries: these galleries are covered by a triple roof: a central one 7 metres high, resting on an outer wall, and on

[1] The Bayon.

columns 2 metres in height; an exterior roof on a double row of columns; and a third resting on a very low wall, pierced with numerous large windows looking on to a narrow interior court.

On the exterior of the wall, which on one side sustains the high roof, are a series of bas-reliefs, surrounding the whole gallery. They are sculptured in the thickness of the wall, and are curious from the scenes and costumes they represent. These scenes are drawn more from the sacred books of the people than from their history; for men with ten heads and twenty arms, fantastic animals, griffins and dragons, are favourite subjects. The men all wear the *langouti*, and often nothing beside, and have the ears pierced and hanging on their shoulders: many have long beards.

In the vestibules of the towers, and in the high galleries near them, are kings and queens seated on a rich dais, with a numerous court, and surrounded by persons carrying parasols, fans, standards, and caskets: there are likewise many musicians with drums, flutes, and harps.

In the galleries are represented several boats' crews fighting; while underneath are fishes disputing for the bodies of the slain. There are also in the same galleries persons in attitudes of adoration, with clasped hands, before a figure of Samanakodom.

In another part is a long procession: the king is in a large open carriage, divided into three compartments, he being in the centre one, and his wives in the two others. This carriage has six wheels and two shafts, which rest on the shoulders of eight men. The chiefs are mounted on elephants or horses, or seated in carriages drawn by four led horses, and by their side march a numerous company bearing standards, parasols, and caskets.

The bas-reliefs at the east and north sides represent similar scenes, as well as many of the fabulous men and animals which are to be seen in those at Ongcor-Wat. In numerous places the water, trickling through holes in the roof, has so obliterated the carving that the subjects can no longer be recognised. This gallery, with its sixteen towers, is connected with another only 3 metres distant; and this last has five towers on each side, of which the three in the middle face the exterior towers. The interior of the gallery with its three roofs receives no light but by the doors, and is so dark that torches are necessary when it is visited. The gallery, sustained by two rows of columns and by an exterior wall, has no bas-reliefs. The towers, which are built at equal distances, are thus disposed: the largest at the angles, two smaller ones next to them, and one of medium size in the centre.

The middle of the terrace is occupied by a large tower connected with the gallery by two others, only about a metre distant. The central tower is circular at the base, is 20 metres in diameter, and nearly 40 metres high, and has on each side a turret. A colonnade supporting a roof, now in ruins, surrounds it: the columns, each of which is hewn out of a single block of stone more than 40 metres high, are still standing. Four doors lead to the interior. Outside this tower, between each two doors, are three chapels, constructed out of the thickness of the wall, and having no communication with each other, nor with the exterior. In nearly every one of them is a full-length statue of Samanakodom seated on a pedestal.

On visiting this place you behold on every side the tops of these numerous towers, and the roofs of the galleries, intermingled with large trees, creepers, and thistles, which invade the courts, the terraces, and other parts; and you have at first some difficulty in comprehending the arrangements of the different buildings. It is only after a long examination that you perceive the symmetry of them as a whole, and that these thirty-seven towers and numerous galleries are all in regular order. Some parts are in good preservation; others have been dealt hardly with by time, in spite of the immense size of the blocks of stone, and the skill with which they are united; and the condition of this stone, ready to crumble to powder, seems to prove that this structure was anterior to Ongcor-Wat.

Like it, it is built of sandstone, and the roofs are very similar, only that, in place of the pointed stones ranged in courses at Ongcor, these are embellished, at about two-thirds of their height, with four gigantic sculptured heads.

The roof is terminated by a very elegant embrasure, a feature not belonging to the other temple. Every door in the building is sunk, and many of them are admirably carved, displaying scenes full of expression, skilfully arranged, and exquisitely delicate in detail. They represent various subjects: worshippers prostrated before their idols, musicians and comedians performing pantomimes, chariots filled with warriors standing up, and drawn by horses galloping: in some instances they appear to be running races.

Not far from this labyrinth are three platforms close together, each occupied by a colossal idol of stone, and gilt. These idols appear to be of modern date; but at their feet are assembled a number of others, some uninjured, some broken, collected from among the ruins. On one of the platforms are several stones fixed in the ground; on one of which is a long undecipherable inscription.

Three walls at some distance from each other, and each bounded by a moat, surround what remains of the palace of the ancient kings.[1] Within the first enclosure are two towers connected by galleries, which form four sides, like a triumphal arch. The walls are of ferruginous stone, and the length of each block forms the thickness of the wall. The towers and galleries are of sandstone.

A hundred metres from the angle of the square formed on the

[1] Phimeanakas

north side by the wall, is a singular building,[1] consisting of two high terraces, and communicating with the outer wall by another terrace half in ruins.

In a cavity recently made by excavations, are visible large sculptured blocks, which seem to have fallen from the top. The walls, still intact, are covered with bas-reliefs, disposed in four rows, one above another, each representing a king seated in the Oriental fashion, with his hands resting on a broken poignard, and by his side a number of women. All these figures are covered with ornaments, such as very long earrings, necklaces, and bracelets. Their costume is the *langouti*, and all wear high head-dresses terminating in a point, and apparently composed of precious stones, pearls, and gold and silver ornaments.

On another side the bas-reliefs represent combats; and here are children with long hair tied up like the savages of the East. Everything here, however, yields in beauty to the statue of the leprous king, which is at the end of the terrace. The head, admirable in its nobility, regularity of feature, and gentle yet proud expression, must have been the work of the most skilful sculptor of the country, in an age when many, doubtless, evinced great talent. A small moustache covers his upper lip, and his hair falls in long curls over his shoulders; but the whole body is naked, and without ornament. One foot and one hand are broken.

About 1200 metres in front of the building just described is one called 'Prea sat sour prot', and said to have been the royal treasury. It is square, and consits of sixteen towers connected by galleries, but nearly all in ruins: the doorways and walls are ornamented with sculpture, as in the other remains. It served, they say, as a depository for the crown jewels. The Cambodians also believe that ropes were stretched from one tower to another, on which dancers

[1] Terrace of the Leper King

exercised their skill in the presence of the king, who, seated on one of the neighbouring terraces, enjoyed their performances. All traditions being lost, the natives invent new ones, according to the measure of their capacity.

The centre of the interior of the third enclosure is occupied by an immense esplanade, supported by walls formed of magnificent blocks of stone, sculptured and surrounded by staircases.[1] The ground is level; but in the excavations that had been made I remarked large masses of carved stone.

Not far from this esplanade is a square building in tolerable preservation, the basement composed of great blocks of ferruginous stone, as are the staircases, of which there are four, one on each side; but they are so steep, narrow, and worn away that it is difficult to climb them. The base supports small galleries, very narrow, and having windows with carved bars. The stones and every doorway are covered with inscriptions.

In the centre of the gallery rises a ruined tower, approached by four staircases, as awkward to ascend as the others just mentioned. Near the doors are some figures of women, standing with flowers in their hands. This building appears very old: the stone is crumbling away like rotten wood.

On the banks of the river which skirts the eastern side of Ongcor Thom are several remains. The first you come to is Fiao Saie;[2] two or three hundred metres from the water's edge. Large and deep ditches surround it on all sides; and when these have been crossed you arrive in front of a terrace 45 metres long, and 2 metres 50 centimetres in width. Four rows of columns 1 metre high are all that is left standing. Those in the middle rows are square, the others are fluted, with capitals. This terrace leads to a square formed by

[1] Terrace of the Elephants
[2] Chau Say Tevoda

four galleries, each 20 metres long: the one facing the terrace has three porticoes with doors and staircases, while in the centre, and at each corner of the gallery, are towers.

Another gallery, 40 metres long, leads from the central tower to another larger one, where, on a high pedestal, is placed the principal idol. On each side of this tower are three staircases, with porticoes projecting four or five metres, and supported by six high columns. All the windows have been ornamented with twisted bars, many of which still remain. By the side of each door are carved columns, every block being cut and polished with infinite patience and art. There are some bas-reliefs portraying a lion devouring a stag, dances, pantomimes, worshippers before idols, &c. As at Ongcor-Wat, the building is entirely composed of great blocks of sand-stone.

Prea sat Iheur Manone Tireada, or the Temple of the Angels,[1] is only about 150 metres from the preceding, and, according to tradition, was formerly a celebrated school for Buddhist theology. At the east is the principal entrance, which consists of a gallery 18 metres long, with a portico in the centre, and staircases. A second gallery, 30 metres long, terminated by a tower, extends from the centre of the other, and at about two-thirds of its length open out on either side porticoes and staircases. There are two other small buildings north and south, and a third behind the tower. That on the south is in good preservation, but receives no light except through a single door. This pagoda has been built with smaller stones than the other temples: in its architecture and details it much resembles Fiao Saie.

Near Iheur Manone Tireada is a bridge of very ancient date,[2] in a fair state of preservation, excepting the parapet and a portion of the roadway, which are a mass of ruins; but the piers and arches

[1] Thommanon
[2] Spean Thma

still remain. The piers are formed of sandstone, some of the blocks being long, others square, and placed irregularly; a few only are carved.

This bridge, with its fourteen narrow arches, may be about 42 or 43 metres in length and 4.5 metres wide.

The river, instead of flowing under its arches, runs now along the side, its bed having been altered by the shifting of the sand, which has so accumulated around the piers and fallen stones, that a great portion of the former is concealed.

This bridge must have served as a communication between Ong-cor the Great and the high road, which, traversing the province from east to west, took afterwards a southerly direction.

Two hundred metres from the bridge rise, amidst the forest, the imposing ruins of Prea sat Kéo,[1] to reach which you have to cross a deep moat. This done, you arrive at the exterior wall, which has four entrances formed by elegant pavilions, with staircases of eight steps leading to a terrace raised nearly 2 metres from the ground; from this you pass into a low narrow gallery with numerous interior windows ornamented with twisted bars. This gallery surrounds the building, and you ascend to it by a staircase leading to a second terrace. Three other terraces, each more than 3 metres 50 centimetres wide, rise one above another, supported on blocks of well-cut sandstone.

Each terrace forms a perfect square, the sides of the first measuring each 30 metres in length. A staircase, 15 metres high and $3\frac{1}{2}$ metres wide, leads to the top; and a wide parapet to the staircase serves as a pedestal for four statues of lions, more or less injured. In the centre of the upper terrace is a lofty tower, and there are four smaller ones at the corners. Each tower has four porticoes with staircases, which rest on a base 7 metres high, and these towers are

[1] Ta Keo

reached by staircases of twenty-two steps. From them a magnificent view is obtained over the surrounding forest. They, as well as their bases and staircases, are built of great blocks of granite arranged in regular tiers, and joined together in the most perfect manner. There is little sculpture, and the doorways have been left unfinished. The towers are without roofs, and perhaps never had any. The whole building appears very ancient, judging by the condition of the stone, which in many places is falling to pieces.

On the road before mentioned are two towns containing some remarkable buildings. These towns, each of which is enclosed by walls forming a square, almost touch each other, being only about 20 metres apart. The walls are of ferruginous stone, surmounted by a coping of carved sandstone resembling a cornice, above which are serrated stones, giving a very finished appearance to the wall.

The smallest of these towns is called Pontéey Kedey (Town of Kedey); the other, Pontéey Ta Proum.

The town of Ta Proum has seven gateways in the style of triumphal arches, formed by a central tower at the entrance and by lateral galleries. As at Ongcor the Great, a deep track is worn in the roadway beneath by the passage of vehicles. The interior of the town is completely deserted; no one enters it except the Cambodians from a hamlet outside the enclosure, who cultivate a few rice-plantations. In the centre are the ruins of a large and splendid monument, which has suffered greatly by the hand of time, and perhaps also from barbarous invasions. The ruins are surrounded by a double wall of ferruginous stone and by deep moats; and at every entrance are galleries with porticoes. A long gallery, 120 metres on each side, and with porticoes at the middle and at each end, goes quite round the building. Exteriorly, on each side, are two detached towers about 10 or 15 metres from the ruins. This gallery is formed by an interior wall and colonnades supporting a vaulted roof, which in many places has fallen in, and most of the columns are over-thrown.

On the opposite wall are large bas-reliefs, forming series of sub-jects, set in a magnificent framework, which is in so good a state of preservation that the delicacy of the execution can be appreciated. As for the bas-reliefs themselves, they are much injured, not so much by time as by some barbarous hand, for everywhere are marks of the hammer or pickaxe. Leaving this gallery on the western side, you enter a long court, in which are three detached towers, and on the opposite side are similar towers.

Several of these, which are from 8 to 10 metres high, and well preserved, are real works of art. The mandarins of the provinces of Ongcor and Battambong are at present occupied in taking two of them to pieces, in order to transport them to Bangkok, the king having issued orders to that effect, and appointed one of the man-darins to carry them out.

Beyond, extends a second rectangular gallery, connected with the first by three parallel galleries and two transverse ones. At the points where they intersect are ten towers, placed, like the galleries, in an odd and unsymmetrical fashion. The perfect preservation of several parts of these last, and the ruinous state of others, seem to mark different ages.

One of the towers and several of the galleries are constructed of ferruginous stone, the others of sandstone. The architecture of the galleries is the same as that of Ongcor-Wat, a double roof with colonnades. All the building is on one floor. This temple, which, after Ongcor-Wat, is the largest of all, is situated in a desert place, and lost amidst a forest; an exuberant vegetation has overgrown everything, galleries and towers, so that it is difficult to force a passage.

IX

THE ANCIENT PEOPLE
OF CAMBODIA

A knowledge of Sanscrit, of 'Pali', and of some modern languages of Hindostan and Indo-China, would be the only means of arriving at the origin of the ancient people of Cambodia who have left all these traces of their civilisation, and that of their successors, who appear only to have known how to destroy, never to reconstruct. Until some learned archaeologist shall devote himself to this subject, it is not probable that aught but contradictory speculations will be promulgated. Some day, however, the truth will surely appear and put them all to flight. I myself, having nothing but conjecture to rest upon, advance my own theory with diffidence.

Nokhor has been the centre and capital of a wealthy, powerful, and civilised state, and in this assertion I do not fear contradiction from those who have any knowledge of its gigantic ruins. Now, for a country to be rich and powerful, a produce relatively great and an extended commerce must be presumed. Doubtless, Cambodia was formerly thus favoured, and would be so at the present day under a wise government, if labour and agriculture were encouraged instead of despised, if the ruling powers exercised a less absolute despotism, and, above all, if slavery were abolished—that miserable institution which is a bar to all progress, reduces man to the level of the brute, and prevents him from cultivating more than sufficient for his own actual wants.

The greater part of the land is surprisingly fertile, and the rice of Battambong is superior to that of Cochin-China. The forests yield precious gums, gum-lac, gamboge, cardamoms, and many others, as well as some useful resins. They likewise produce most valuable timber, both for home use and for exportation, and dye-woods in great variety. The mines afford gold, iron, and copper.

Fruits and vegetables of all kinds abound, and game is in great profusion. Above all, the great lake is a source of wealth to the whole nation; the fish in it are so incredibly abundant that when the water is high they are actually crushed under the boats, and the play of the oars is frequently impeded by them. The quantities taken there every year by a number of enterprising Cochin-Chinese are literally miraculous. The river of Battambong is not less plentifully stocked, and I have seen a couple of thousand taken in one net.

Neither must I omit to mention the various productions which form so important a part of the riches of a nation, and which might be here cultivated in the greatest perfection. I would especially instance cotton, coffee, indigo, tobacco, and the mulberry, and such spices as nutmegs, cloves, and ginger. Even now all these are grown to a certain limited extent, and are allowed to be of superior quality. Sufficient cotton is raised to supply all Cochin-China, and to allow of some being exported to China itself. From the little island of Ko-Sutin alone, leased to the planters by the King of Cambodia, the transport of the cotton produce employs a hundred vessels. What might not be accomplished if these were colonies belonging to a country such, for example, as England, and were governed as are the dependencies of that great and generous nation?

Battambong and Korat are renowned for their silken 'langoutis' of brilliant and varied colours, both the material and the dyes being the produce of the country.

A glance at the map of Cambodia suffices to show that it communicates with the sea by the numerous mouths of the Mekon and the numberless canals of Lower Cochin-China, which was formerly subject to it; with Laos and with China, by the great river.

These facts being established, whence came the original inhabitants of this country? Was it from India, the cradle of civilisation, or was it from China? The language of the present natives is that of the old Cambodians or Khendome, as they call the people who live retired at the foot of the mountains and on the table-lands, and it is too distinct from Chinese to render the latter supposition possible. But whether this people originally came from the north or from the west, by sea, and gradually making their way up the rivers, or from the land, and descending them, it seems certain that there must have been here other ancient settlers, who introduced Buddhism and civilisation. It would appear as though these had been succeeded by some barbarous race, who drove the original inhabitants far into the interior, and destroyed many of their buildings. At all events, it is my belief that, without exaggeration, the date of some of the oldest parts of Ongcor the Great may be fixed at more than 2000 years ago, and the more recent portions not much later. The state of decay of many of these structures would indicate even a greater age; but they probably date from the dispersion of the Indian Buddhists, which took place several centuries before the Christian era, and which led to the expatriation of thousands of individuals.

All that can be said respecting the present Cambodians is, that they are an agricultural people, among whom a certain taste for art still shows itself in the carved work of the boats belonging to the better classes, and their chief characteristic is unbounded conceit.

It is not so among the savages of the east, called by the Cambodians their elder brothers. I passed four months among them,[1] and, arriving direct from Cambodia, it seemed like entering a country comparatively civilised. Great gentleness, politeness, and even sociability—which, to my fancy, bore evidence of a past refinement —struck me in these poor children of nature, buried for centuries in their deep forests, which they believe to be the largest portion of the world, and to which they are so strongly attached that no inducement would tempt them to move.

When looking at the figures in the bas-reliefs at Ongcor, I could

[1] See Chapter VI above.

not avoid remarking the strong resemblance of the faces to those of these savages. And besides the similar regularity of feature, there are the same long beards, straight *langoutis*, and even the same weapons and musical instruments.

I myself remarked many Stiên words like the Cambodian, especially in the western districts, where there exists some commerce between the two countries. To all this must be added that the Siamese, Laotian, and Cambodian seem to be sister languages: more than a fourth part of the words, especially those expressing intellectual things, are exactly the same in each.

The mountains of Dom-rêe, situated a little way to the north of Ongcor, are inhabited by a gentle and inoffensive race, although looked upon as savages by their brethren of the plain. These latter are the Somrais: they speak the Cambodian language, but with a different pronunciation. Beyond are the provinces, formerly belonging to Cambodia, but now Siamese.

According to popular belief, the king, if he should cross the great lake, is sure to die in the course of the year.

Whilst the present sovereign was prince he paid a visit to Ongcor, and seeing some of the Somrais, said, 'These are my true subjects, and the stock from which my family sprang.' It seems that, in fact, the present dynasty did so.

The Cambodians give the following account of the introduction of Buddhism among them. Samanakodom left Ceylon and went to Thibet, where he was very well received; from thence he went among the savages, but, not meeting with encouragement from them, he took refuge in Cambodia, where he was welcomed by the people.

A circumstance worthy of remark is that the name of Rome is familiar to nearly all the Cambodians: they pronounce it Rouma, and place it at the western end of the world.

I have written these few notes on Cambodia, after returning from a long hunting expedition, by the light of a torch, seated on my tiger-skin. On one side of me is the skin of an ape just stripped off; on the other, a box of insects waiting to be arranged and packed; and my employment has not been rendered easier by the sanguinary attacks of mosquitoes and leeches. My desire is, not to impose my opinions on any one, especially with regard to the wonderful architectural remains which I have visited, but simply to disclose the existence of these monuments, which are certainly the most gigantic, and also to my mind display a more perfect taste than any left to us by the ancients; and, moreover, to collect all the facts and traditions possible about these countries, hoping they may be useful to explorers of greater talent and fortune. For, I doubt not, others will follow in my steps, and, aided by their own government and by that of Siam, advantages denied to myself, will gather an abundant harvest where I have but cleared the ground.

But, after all, my principal object is natural history, and with that study I chiefly occupy myself. I have written, as I said before, in leisure hours, when resting from my fatigues, with a desire to implant in the breasts of others a love for the great works of Nature, and to benefit those who, in the quiet of their homes, delight to follow the poor traveller; who, often with the sole object of being useful to his fellow-men, or of discovering some insect, plant, or unknown animal, or verifying some point of latitude, crosses the ocean, and sacrifices family, comfort, health, and, too often, life itself.

But it is pleasant to the man devoted to our good and beautiful mother, Nature, to think that his work, his fatigues, his troubles and dangers, are useful to others, if not to himself. Nature has her lovers, and those alone who have tasted them know the joys she gives. I candidly confess that I have never been more happy than when amidst this grand and beautiful tropical scenery, in the profound solitude of these dense forests, the stillness only broken by the song of birds and the cries of wild animals; and even if destined here to meet my death, I would not change my lot for all the joys and pleasures of the civilised world.

After a sojourn of three weeks within the walls of Ongcor-Wat in order to make drawings and plans, I returned to Battambong. The principal ruins of this province are those of Bassette, Banone, and Watêk. I visited Bassette twice, before going to Ongcor and after. The whole place is so ruinous, that one might suppose some enemy had done his utmost to demolish it, or that one gazed at the results of an earthquake. Ascending the river for about forty miles from Battambong in a southerly direction, you arrive at a mountain standing somewhat isolated, but forming part of the ramifications of the great chain of Pursat. At the foot is a miserable pagoda of recent origin, and in the environs a few hamlets, while on the summit are the ruins of Banone. Eight towers are connected with galleries, and communicate on two sides by a wall with a central tower nearly 8 metres in diameter. Although there is nothing about them especially remarkable, what remains of the galleries displays fine workmanship, and great taste and skill in construction. Wat-Ek is situated in an immense plain, bounded north and east by the beautiful mountains of Pursat and ramifications of those of Chantaboun. The architecture of the galleries is full of beauty, and that of the tower very imposing; but neither here nor at Banone are you met by the singular grandeur and magnificence which make so great an impression on you in visiting Ongcor and most of the other ruins.

I inquired for some means of transport to Bangkok, but, on different pretexts, I was detained more than two months before I could get away, in spite of the assistance of the viceroy. At last, on the 5th March, I set off with two waggons and two pair of powerful buffaloes, which had been taken wild, and trained up to the yoke, and were strong enough to sustain the fatigues of a journey at this season.

This time I carried along with me a complete menagerie; but of all my prisoners a pretty young chimpanzee, which, after slightly wounding it, we had succeeded in taking alive, was the most amusing. As long as I kept him in my room, and he could amuse himself with the numerous children and other visitors whom curiosity brought to look at him, he was very gentle; but as I was obliged on the journey to fasten him at the back of one of the waggons, he became frightened, and used every effort to break his chain, continually screaming, and trying to hide himself. After a time, however, he got accustomed to his position, and was quiet and docile as before.

Our guns on our shoulders, I and my young Chinese Phrai followed or walked before the waggons, occasionally finding some sport as we skirted the forest. As for my other servant, when we had reached Pinhalu,[1] he begged to be allowed to return to Bangkok by our former route; so, not wishing to retain him against his will, I had paid his expenses home, and wished him happiness.

Scarcely had we proceeded a mile when our drivers asked my permission to stop for supper, saying that afterwards we could set out again, and travel part of the night. I at once consented, knowing it to be a custom with the Cambodians, before departing on a long journey, to make their first halt not far from their village, that they may return home to shed a last tear, and partake of a farewell glass.

Before the oxen were even unyoked, the families of our drivers were all collected round me, the whole party talking at once, and

[1] The journey to and from Brelum was evidently too much for Niou.

begging me to take care of their relations, to save them from robbers, and give them medicine if they had a headache. They all then took their evening meal together, washing it down with some glasses of arrack which I gave them; after which we resumed our journey by a magnificent moonlight, but treading in a bed of dust which reached to our ankles, and raised a thick cloud round our waggons.

X

PREPARATIONS

ON the 4th April I returned to Bangkok, after fifteen months' absence. During the greater part of this time I had never known the comfort of sleeping in a bed; and throughout my wanderings my only food had been rice or dried fish, and I had not once tasted good water. I was astonished at having preserved my health so well, particularly in the forests, where, often wet to the skin, and without a change of clothes, I have had to pass whole nights by a fire at the foot of a tree; yet I have not had a single attack of fever, and been always happy and in good spirits, especially when lucky enough to light upon some novelty. A new shell or insect filled me with a joy which ardent naturalists alone can understand; but they know well how little fatigues and privations of all kinds are cared for when set against the delight experienced in making one discovery after another, and in feeling that one is of some slight assistance to the votaries of science. It pleases me to think that my investigations into the archaeology, entomology, and conchology of these lands may be of use to certain members of the great and generous English nation, who kindly encouraged the poor naturalist; whilst France, his own country, remained deaf to his voice.

It was another great pleasure to me, after these fifteen months of travelling, during which very few letters from home had reached me, to find, on arriving at Bangkok, an enormous packet, telling me all the news of my distant family and country. It is indeed happiness, after so long a period of solitude, to read the lines traced by the beloved hands of an aged father, of a wife, of a brother. These joys are to be reckoned among the sweetest and purest of life.

We stopped in the centre of the town, at the entrance of a canal, whence there is a view over the busiest part of the Menam. It was almost night, and silence reigned around us; but when at daybreak I rose and saw the ships lying at anchor in the middle of the stream, while the roofs of the palaces and pagodas reflected the first rays of the sun, I thought that Bangkok had never looked so beautiful.

I had intended to visit the north-east of the country of Laos, crossing Dong Phya Phai (the forest of the King of Fire), and going on to Hieng Naie, on the frontiers of Cochin-China; thence to the confines of Tonquin. I had planned to return afterwards by the Mekon to Cambodia, and then to pass through Cochin-China, should the arms of France have been victorious there. However, the rainy season having commenced, the whole country was inundated, and the forests impassable; so it was necessary to wait four months before I could put my project in execution. I therefore packed up and sent off all my collections, and after remaining a few weeks in Bangkok I departed for Pechaburi, situated about 13° north lat., and to the north of the Malayan peninsula.

After a sojourn of four months among the mountains of Pechaburi, I returned to Bangkok to make the necessary preparations for my new expedition to the north-east of Laos, my intended route being to the basin of the Mekon, toward the frontier of China. I had an additional motive for coming here again, namely, to get cured of that annoying complaint the itch, which I caught at Pechaburi; how, I really cannot guess, for, in spite of the mosquitoes, I bathed regularly two or three times a day; but I hope that a short course of rubbing with sulphur ointment, and proper baths, will effect a cure. This, one of the ills of a traveller's life, is, however, trifling in comparison with the misfortune of which I have just heard. The steamer 'Sir James Brooke', in which Messrs. Gray, Hamilton, and Co., of Singapore, had sent off all my last boxes of collections, has foundered at the entrance of that port. And so all my poor insects, which have cost me so much care and pains for many months, are lost for ever—some of them rare and valuable specimens, which, alas! I shall probably never be able to replace.

I have waited till the last moment[1] for the steamer which ought to bring me letters from Europe, but unfortunately I am obliged to set out without receiving any answers to those which I sent in May, on my return from Cambodia. I fear that, once in the interior of the country, I shall have no means of sending letters; arm yourself, therefore, with patience, dear brother, and do not think me neglectful if you do not receive any; but be sure that I, alone in those profound solitudes, shall suffer more than you, from my ignorance of everything concerning those dear to me; and during the eighteen or twenty months which the journey will probably occupy I shall not see a European face nor hear a word which can recall to me my beloved country.

I have done everything in my power to obtain letters and passports from the French and Siamese authorities here, but all have been nearly useless. I have obtained nothing but a letter from the King's brother, who has the superintendence of the provinces north of Laos, and with that I trust to be able to get on. The good Dr. Campbell has supplied me with medicines of all kinds, and as I am nearly acclimatized, and have with me devoted followers—one particularly, Phrai, who would die for me—you may be easy on my account. Besides, and I really know not why, I have hitherto been much liked by the missionaries and natives, and I am sure it will be the same there. Fever does not kill all travellers. I have traversed many dangerous districts in my journey to Cambodia, and I am safe. Let us trust in God, my brother, that I shall be as fortunate in this expedition, and that we shall meet again. Nothing is requisite but courage, hope, and patience. I am sober, and drink nothing but tea. My food is the same as that of the natives, dried fish and rice, and sometimes a little game which I shoot, and roast

[1] This paragraph and the next one ending with the words 'Adieu, my brother!' are taken from Mouhot's letter to his brother Charles dated 13th October, 1860.

on a spit after the fashion of the natives, that is, by two bamboos stuck into the ground and another laid horizontally on them, which is turned from time to time. My amusements are hunting, arranging my collections, my drawings, to which I devote a great deal of time, and of which some are not bad, as you may judge by those sent to the Geographical Society of London, and my journal; with those I pass many pleasant hours. Besides, you know how I love nature, and am only really happy in the woods with my gun, and that when there, if I know you all to be happy, I have nothing to wish for. I often think of our good old father, but as long as you are with him I feel easy about him; you will make him bear my absence patiently, repeat often to him how I love him, and how happy I shall be when I can tell him about my long journeys. And you, my brother, love and cherish your two dear children, my little nephews; inculcate in them the love of nature, and teach them to think that virtue is recompensed even here, and a good conscience ennobles more than patents of nobility, or orders in the button-hole; bring up your little ones in the love of God, and of all that is good and great. Think and talk sometimes with Jenny of the poor traveller. Adieu, my brother!

My friend M. Malherbes accompanied me for a few hours' sail from Bangkok, and then we parted with a warm clasp of the hand, and, I confess, not without tears in both our eyes, trusting that destiny might reunite us here or elsewhere. My friend's light boat glided rapidly down the stream; in a few minutes he was out of sight, and I was again left alone—for how long a period being quite uncertain. I know what awaits me, having been warned both by the missionaries and the natives. During the last twenty-five years, only one man, as far as I know, a French priest, has penetrated to the heart of Laos, and he only returned to die in the arms of the good and venerable prelate, Mgr. Pallegoix. I know the discomfort, fatigue, and tribulations of all sorts to which I am again about to expose myself; the want of roads, the difficulty of finding means of conveyance, and the risk of paying for the slightest imprudence by a dangerous or even fatal illness. And how can one be prudent when compelled to submit to the hardest life of the forest, to suffer many privations, and to brave all inclemencies of the weather? Nevertheless, my destiny urges me on, and I trust in the kind Providence which has watched over me until now.

Only a few hours before my departure from Bangkok, the mail arrived, and I received news of my dearly loved family, which consoled me for the misfortune I sustained in the loss of my collections. Thanks, thanks, my good friends, for the pleasure you gave me before starting, by the expression of your warm and constant affection; I shall not forget you in my solitude.

I shall continue during my journey to take notes of all my little adventures, very rare, alas! for I am not one of those travellers who kill a tiger and an elephant at one shot; the smallest unknown shell or insect is more interesting to me; however, on occasion, I do not object to a meeting with the terrible inhabitants of the forest, and more than one have known the range of my rifle and the calibre of my balls.

Every evening, enclosed in my mosquito curtains, either in some cabin or at the foot of a tree, in the jungle or by the river bank, I shall talk to you, my friends; you shall be the companions of my journey, and it will be my greatest pleasure to confide to you my impressions and thoughts.

Scarcely had my friend M. Malherbes left me, when I discovered, in the bottom of my boat, a box, which he had contrived to place, unknown to me, among my packages; a fresh proof of his kindness, for he had already sent me three cases when I was at Pechaburi. I found it to contain some dozens of Bordeaux, as much cognac, boxes of sardines, biscuits, and a number of other things, which would recall to me, were I ever likely to forget it, the true and considerate friendship of my countrymen, so valuable to one far from home.

Let me say, in passing, that I am cured of the itch, which I suspect my servants had caught in wandering about the villages, and had communicated to me, in spite of my scrupulous cleanliness.

I have four Laotian rowers; one of them was in my service for a month two years ago, and he now begged to be allowed to attend me throughout my journey, telling me I should find him very useful. After a little hesitation I have engaged him, so now I shall have three servants. My good and faithful Phrai has never left me, luckily for me, for I should find it difficult to replace him; and, besides, I am attached to the lad, who is active, intelligent, industrious, and devoted to me. Deng—which means 'The Red'—his companion, is another Chinese whom I brought from Pechaburi. He is very useful to me as interpreter, especially when I wish to comprehend persons who speak with a great piece of betel between their teeth. He is likewise my cook, and shows his skill when we want to add an additional dish to our ordinary fare, which occasionally happens when some unfortunate stag comes within range of my gun, or I bring down a pigeon, or even a monkey, a kind of game not much to my taste, though highly esteemed by my Chinese, as well as wild dog and rat. Every one to his taste.

This attendant of mine has one little defect, but who has not in this world? He now and then takes a drop too much, and I have often found him sucking, through a bamboo cane, the spirit of wine from one of the bottles in which I preserve my reptiles, or laying under contribution the cognac presented to me by my friend Malherbes. A few days ago he was seized with this devouring thirst, and, profiting by my absence for only a few minutes, he opened my chest, and hastily laid hands on the first bottle which presented itself, great part of the contents of which he swallowed at one gulp. I came back just as he was wiping his mouth with his shirt-sleeve, and it would be impossible to describe his contortions and grimaces as he screamed out that he was poisoned.

He had had the bad luck to get hold of my bottle of ink; his face was smeared with it, and his shirt pretty well sprinkled. It was a famous lesson for him, and I think it will be some time before he tries my stores again.

I soon reached the mountains of Nephaburi and Phrabat, with their pure clear atmoshpere, the weather being pleasant and a fresh wind blowing. All nature looks smiling, and I feel exhilarated and happy. Here my heart dilates, and I could fancy I had grown ever so much taller since I arrived. Here I can breathe, I live, amid these beautiful hills and woods; in cities I seem to suffocate, and the sight of so great a number of human beings annoys me.

Beetles of the longicorn tribe abound here; and to-day I have filled a box with more than a thousand new or rare insects. I have even been fortunate enough to replace some of the more valuable kinds which were destroyed or injured by sea-water on board the 'Sir James Brooke'. The villagers come every day to bring me 'beasts', as they call them, grasshoppers, scorpions, serpents, tortoises, &c., all presented to me at the end of a stick.

At last we breathe a pure and delicious air. It is now mid winter; since the day before yesterday a fresh north wind has blown, and at night the thermometer has gone back to $18°$ centigrade. All the evening I have been walking by the river, wrapped in a warm burnous, with the hood up. Phrai and Deng wear their whole wardrobe both night and day, and I have seen them dressed in red flannel and with felt hats, when you might take them for Garibaldians, as far, that is to say, as their costume is concerned, for their appearance otherwise is far from warlike; however, they are not wanting in a kind of courage which has its own merit. They dance and sing round a good fire, and open their eyes with astonishment when I tell them that I have seen rivers larger than the Menam frozen over so hard that the heaviest vehicles could go upon them with safety, and others on which whole oxen have been roasted; and that men and animals often die of cold.

My little 'Tine-Tine' says nothing, but creeps under my counterpane and sleeps at his ease; only if Phrai torments him by lifting the cover, he shows his teeth. Ungrateful being that I am, I have not yet spoken of this little companion who is so faithful and attached to me—of this pretty 'King Charles', whom I brought from home. All the Siamese, and especially those who have no children, are very fond of the little creature, notwithstanding their general aversion for dogs. Theirs, however, are usually half savage. I much fear that my poor dog will come to an untimely end, and be trampled under foot by some elephant, or devoured at a mouthful by a tiger.

Every day we go out on our collecting expeditions; but while we are seeking insects or birds, the sound of our voices, or the report of our guns, repeated by the mountain echoes, brings forth the wild beasts from their dens. Yesterday, after a long and fatiguing excursion, during which we had killed some birds and one or two monkeys, we were returning home quite worn out, when we reached a small clearing in the forest, and here I told my two boys to take a little repose at the foot of a tree, while I went to hunt for insects.

Suddenly I heard a sound as of some animal gliding through the thick underwood. I looked round, at the same time loading my gun, and then crept quietly back to the tree where my servants lay asleep, when I perceived a large and beautiful leopard taking his spring to clear the brushwood, and pounce upon one of them as he lay all unconscious. I fired, the shot striking the animal in the right shoulder. He gave a tremendous leap, and rolled over among the bushes, which much embarassed his movements. However, he was but wounded, and still dangerous, if my second ball did not kill, or at least cripple him. I fired again, and hit him between the shoulders; the ball lodged in the heart, and he fell dead almost instantaneously. The terror of my two poor followers, suddenly awakened by the report of my gun so close to their ears, was only equalled by their pleasure when they saw the creature extended lifeless before them.

Another year has flown, a year chequered for me, as for others, with joy, anxiety, and trouble; and to-day my thoughts turn especially to the few who are dear to me.

You know my manner of life, so I shall not repeat it.[1] The heat and the mosquitoes make a real hell of this place. Those who praise it must have hard heads and skins, or else must be comfortably lodged, and surrounded by an army of slaves. They know nothing but its enjoyments. If there is one pleasant hour in the morning and another in the evening, one must think oneself lucky, for often there is no peace night or day. My pleasures are, first, liberty, that precious thing without which man cannot be happy, and for which so many have fought and will fight still; then, seeing so much that is beautiful, grand, and new, and which no one has seen before me. From these I draw my contentment. Thank God! my health is as good as when I left you, although three years have passed over me.

Soon I shall be in Laos, and then, what strange things I shall see daily! what curious beings I shall meet, to whom I shall be equally an object of curiosity! I shall have delightful days, then, perhaps,

---

[1] This and the next four paragraphs are taken from a letter written by Mouhot to his sister-in-law on 21st December 1860.

sad ones, if my servants have the fever, which happens at intervals. If only to enliven these solitudes, I could have you here, my dear Jenny, or if I could sing like you, or even like a nightingale! Sometimes I do make use of my falsetto voice, and hum the beautiful airs of Béranger, and feel strengthened by the sublime odes of that great man of genius.

Two or three thin volumes—I say thin, for the white ants have eaten the greater part of them—and a few old newspapers (new to me) compose my library; but I have blank paper, which I fill as I best can; it is an amusement, at least; and if it turn out of no other use than to serve to amuse you all, I shall be satisfied, for I am not ambitious. I dream as I smoke my pipe, for I must confess that I smoke more than ever.

Well! the mosquitoes and thorns will still be my companions for a long time. It is my own choice, and I shall never complain as long as God grants to all of you the joy and happiness I wish for you.

How I shall accomplish the long journey before me I know not; probably with oxen and elephants; but if even I have to go on foot I care not, so that I reach there, for I have determined to drive away even the devil, should I meet him here.

From more than one loving heart arise, I feel sure, on this day, good wishes for the poor traveller, and from no one more warmly than from you, my dear father. You long for my return; so writes my brother in his last letter, forwarded to me from Bangkok. But I am only commencing my new campaign; would it be like a good soldier to leave on the eve of the engagement? I am at the gates of the infernal regions, for so the Laotians and Siamese designate this forest, and I have no spell to terrify the demons which inhabit it, neither tiger's teeth nor stunted stag-horn; nothing but my faith in and love for God. If I must die here, where so many other wanderers have left their bones, I shall be ready when my hour comes.

The profound stillness of this forest, and its luxuriant tropical vegetation, are indescribable, and at this midnight hour impress me deeply. The sky is serene, the air fresh, and the moon's rays only penetrate here and there, through the foliage, in patches, which appear on the ground like pieces of white paper dispersed by the wind. Nothing breaks the silence but a few dead leaves rustling to the earth, the murmur of a brook which flows over its pebbly bed at my feet, and the frogs answering each other on either side, and whose croaking resembles the hoarse barking of a dog. Now and then I can distinguish the flapping of the bats, attracted by the flame of the torch which is fastened to a branch of the tree under which my tiger-skin is spread; or, at longer intervals, the cry of some panther calling to its mate, and responded to from the tree-tops by the growling of the chimpanzees, whose rest the sound has disturbed.

With a sabre in one hand and a torch in the other, Phrai pursues the fishes in the stream, and he and his shadow reflected on the rocks and water, as he stands there making sudden darts, and crying out 'hit' or 'missed', might easily be mistaken by the natives for demons.

I cannot shake off a feeling of sadness which a few hours of sleep and a long chase to-morrow will probably dissipate; yet, at the moment, I cannot forbear asking myself, how will this year end for me? And you, my dear father, be not too anxious as to my fate, but preserve that tranquillity, hope, and love of God, which alone can make men strong and great: with this help and support, our reunion will not be long delayed. Courage then, and hope! our perseverance and efforts will be recompensed. And thou, invisible link, which, in spite of distance, unites hearts, bear to all those dear to me a thousand embraces, and fill them with all those thoughts

133

which at all times give me strength, and supply joy and consolation in my saddest and most dreary hours. To all, then, a happy new year! and may I bring back safe and sound my poor young followers, who have been such faithful and devoted companions; and who, although already rather weakened by fever and incipient dysentery, are still full of gaiety and energy, and as much attached to me as ever.

XI

JOURNEY INTO LAOS

You will be astonished, my dear friend, to see my letter dated from Saraburi, instead of from Laos.[1] When I reached Chaiapume, I went to the governor with my letters, and asked him to lend me elephants to enable me to continue my journey, that being the only method of travelling among these mountains; but he refused me decidedly, and consequently I have been forced to retrace my steps. Here one can do nothing without the help of the people in power.

I therefore returned to Korat, and established Phrai in a hut which I hired of a Chinese; and went myself to Bangkok, to procure from the authorities orders to the different governors of provinces to aid me instead of throwing obstacles in my way.

From Korat I had the pleasure of travelling with an amiable mandarin of Bangkok, who had been to fetch a white elephant from Laos, and who had conceived a great friendship for me. He travelled in great style; the caravan was magnificent; we had more than sixty elephants, two of which were placed at my disposal, one for my own use, and one for my servants.

Finding myself in the good graces of this mandarin, I told him why I was going to Bangkok, and he promised to obtain for me all I wanted.

When I reached Saraburi I found all the governors of Laos and the first mandarins of Bangkok assembled there to take care of the white elephant. The Siamese, being very superstitious, and believing in metempsychosis, think that the soul of some prince or king has passed into the white elephant; they have the same belief as to white apes and albinoes, consequently they hold them all in great respect. They do not worship them, for the Siamese recognise no God, not

[1] This and the succeeding six paragraphs are taken from a letter which Mouhot wrote to his brother from Saraburi on 24th February 1861.

even Buddha, but they believe that a white elephant brings luck to the country.

During the whole journey the men were busy cutting down branches to make his passage easy; two mandarins fed him with different kinds of cakes in golden dishes, and the King came out to meet him.

I owe, therefore, to the white elephant the most satisfactory letters which I have obtained, and which have cost me my best gun and nearly 300 francs in presents; but I might have had to give much more, and, as I am going to Bangkok, I can replenish my stock. As for the poor elephant, he was so much cared for and so well fed, that he died of indigestion.

I left Bangkok once more, after having experienced for a fortnight the kind hospitality of my friend Dr. Campbell, one of the best men I ever met with: his goodness, friendliness, and British frankness, won my heart and my esteem. After all this loss of time and great expense I went again to Korat, where I was well received by the governor; and he gave me, in addition to my other letters, one for the mandarins of all provinces under his jurisdiction, commanding them to furnish me with as many oxen and elephants as I might require. The greater part of the inhabitants, with Phrai at their head, came out to meet me, and several gave me presents—sacks of rice, fish, fruits, or tobacco, all in abundance.

Two Chinese in our caravan arrived at Korat in a frightful state of fever. One I was able to save by administering quinine in good time, but the other, who appeared the strongest, was dead almost as soon as I heard of his being ill.

I went to see a temple nine miles east of Korat, called Penom-Wat. It is very remarkable, although much inferior in grandeur and beauty to those of Ongcor. The second governor lent me a pony and guide, and, after crossing extensive rice plantations, under a vertical and fiery sun, we reached the spot to which my curiosity had attracted me, and which, like an oasis, could be recognised a long way off by the freshness of its coconut-trees and its rich verdure. I did not arrive there, however, without having taken an involuntary bath. In crossing the Tekon, which is nearly four feet deep, I, in order to escape a wetting, tried to imitate Franconi, by standing on my saddle; but, unluckily, according to the custom of the country, this was fastened on by two pieces of string, and in the middle of the stream it turned and sent me head foremost into the water. But there was no worse result from the accident than my having to remain for half an hour afterwards dressed in Siamese fashion.

Penom-Wat is an interesting temple 36 metres long by 40 wide, and the plan resembles a cross with tolerable exactness. It is composed of two pavilions, with vaulted stone roofs and elegant porticoes. The roofs are from seven to eight metres in height, the gallery three metres wide in the interior, and the walls a metre thick. At each façade of the gallery are two windows with twisted bars.

This temple is built of red and grey sandstone, coarse in the grain, and in some places beginning to decay. On one of the doors is a long inscription, and above are sculptures representing nearly the same subjects as those at Ongcor and Bassette.

In one of the pavilions are several Buddhist idols in stone, the largest of which is 2 metres 50 centimetres high, and actually covered with rags.

You might here easily imagine yourself among the ruins of Ongcor. There is the same style of architecture, the same taste displayed, the same immense blocks polished like marble, and so beautifully fitted together, that I can only compare it to the joining and planing of so many planks.

The whole building is, without doubt, the work of the Khmer-dom, and not an imitation, and must be as old as the illustrious reigns which have left the traces of their grandeur in different parts of the empire. The exterior is not equal to the interior. Penom was the temple of the Queen, so say the Siamese; that of the King, her husband, is at Pimaie, a district about 30 miles east of Korat.

To consult any existing maps of Indo-China for my guidance in the interior of Laos would have been a folly, no traveller, at least to my knowledge, having penetrated into east Laos, or published any authentic information respecting it. To question the natives about places more than a degree distant would have been useless. My desire was to reach Louang-Prabang by land, to visit the northern tribes dependent on that state, and then again to descend the Mekon to Cambodia. Setting out from Korat, I had but to proceed northwards as long as I found practicable roads and inhabited places; and if I could not go by a direct route to Louang-Prabang, I should only have to diverge to the east when I judged it necessary.

I was again delayed a few days at Korat before I could obtain elephants, in consequence of the absence of the viceroy; but on his return he received me in a friendly manner, and gave me a letter of introduction to the governors of the provinces under his jurisdiction. He likewise furnished me with two elephants for myself and servants, and two others for my baggage; so at last I was able to set out for Chaiapume. Before I started, the Chinese with whom I lodged gave me the following advice:—'Buy a tam-tam, and, wherever you halt, sound it. They will say, "Here is an officer of the king"; robbers will keep aloof, and the authorities will respect you. If this does not answer, the only plan to get rid of all the difficulties which the Laotian officials will be sure to throw in you way is to have a good stick, the longer the better. Try it on the back of any mandarin who makes the least resistance and will not do what you wish. Put all delicacy aside. Laos is not like a country of the whites. Follow my advice, and you will find it good.'

I was, however, much better received on my second visit to Chaiapume, and required neither tam-tam nor cane. The sight of the elephants and the order from the viceroy of Korat made the mandarin as supple as a glove, and he provided me with other elephants for a visit to some ruins existing about 3 leagues north of the town, at the foot of a mountain. The superstitious Laotians say that these ruins contain gold, but that every one who has sought for it has been struck with madness.

Two roads lead from Chaiapume to Poukiéan; the first, across the mountains, is so excessively difficult, that I decided on taking the other, which, however, is much longer. The first day we started at 1 o'clock, and reached a village named Non Jasiea, where we were overtaken by a fearful storm. We sheltered ourselves as well as we could, and arrived before night at the entrance of a forest where we slept.

For five days we were compelled to remain in the forest on account of the weather; it rained a great part of the day, and throughout the night; the torrents overflowed, and the earth was nothing but a sea of mud. I never in my life passed such wretched nights, as all the time we had to remain with our wet clothes on our backs, and I cannot describe what we suffered. The snow hurricanes, so frequent in Russia, and which nearly killed me when in that country, seemed trifling miseries in comparison. My poor Phrai was seized with a dreadful fever two days before reaching Poukiéan, and I myself felt very ill.

The passage of the mountains was easy, and the ascent very gradual; blocks of stone obstruct the road in various parts, but our oxen and elephants made their way without much difficulty. I had bought a horse for myself at Korat. During the journey one of my chests was thrown to the ground by the movements of the elephant, and broken to pieces, as, unfortunately, were all the contents, consisting of instruments, and bottles of spirit of wine containing serpents and fishes.

Poukiéan is a smaller village than Chaiapume. Poverty and misery reign here; we cannot find even a fish to purchase; nothing but rice; and as soon as my faithful Phrai is on his legs again we shall leave the place.

Tine-tine attracts the most attention. The people do not, as we pass, cry out first, 'Look at the white stranger,' but 'A little dog!' and every one runs to see this curiosity. My turn comes afterwards.

In all this mountainous region elephants are the only means of transport. Every village possesses some, several as many as fifty or a hundred. Without this intelligent animal no communication would be possible during seven months of the year, while, with his assistance, there is scarcely a place to which you are unable to penetrate.

The elephant ought to be seen on these roads, which I can only call devil's pathways, and are nothing but ravines, ruts two or three feet deep, full of mud; sometimes sliding with his feet close together on the wet clay of the steep slopes, sometimes half buried in mire, an instant afterwards mounted on sharp rocks, where one would think a Blondin alone could stand; striding across enormous trunks of fallen trees, crushing down the smaller trees and bamboos which oppose his progress, or lying down flat on his stomach that the cornacs (drivers) may the easier place the saddle on his back; a hundred times a day making his way, without injuring them, between trees where there is barely room to pass; sounding with his trunk the depth of the water in the streams or marshes; constantly kneeling down and rising again, and never making a false step. It is necessary, I repeat, to see him at work like this in his own country, to form any idea of his intelligence, docility, and strength, or how all those wonderful joints of his are adapted to their work—fully to understand that this colossus is no rough specimen of nature's handiwork, but a creature of especial amiability and sagacity, designed for the service of man.

We must not, however, exaggerate his merits. Probably the saddles used by the Laotians are capable of great improvement; but I must admit that the load of three small oxen, that is to say, about 250 or 300 pounds, is all that I ever saw the largest elephants carry easily, and 18 miles is the longest distance they can accomplish with an ordinary load. Ten or twelve miles are the usual day's work. With four, five, or sometimes seven elephants, I travelled over all the mountain country from the borders of Laos to Louang-Prabang, a distance of nearly 500 miles.

Most of the villages are situated about a day's journey from one another, but frequently you have to travel for three or four days without seeing a single habitation, and then you have no alternative but to sleep in the jungle. This might be pleasant in the dry season, but, during the rains, nothing can give an idea of the sufferings of travellers at night, under a miserable shelter of leaves hastily spread over a rough framework of branches, assaulted by myriads of mosquitoes attracted by the light of the fires and torches, by legions of ox-flies, which, after sunset, attack human beings as well as elephants, and by fleas so minute as to be almost invisible, which assemble about you in swarms, and whose bites are excessively painful, and raise enormous blisters.

To these enemies add the leeches, which, after the least rain, come out of the ground, scent a man twenty feet off, and hasten to suck his blood with wonderful avidity. To coat your legs with a layer of lime when travelling is the only way to prevent them covering your whole body.

Since leaving Korat I have crossed five large rivers which fall into the Mekon, the bed of which is more or less full according to the season. The first of these, 35 metres wide, is called the Menam Chie, lat. 15°45'; second, the Menam Leuye, 90 metres wide, lat. 18°3'; third, the Menam Ouan, at Kenne-Tao, 100 metres in width, lat. 18°35'; fourth, the Nam Pouye, 60 metres, lat. 19°; fifth, the Nam-Houn, 80 or 100 metres wide, lat. 20°.

The Chie is navigable, as far up as the latitude of Korat, from May to December; the Leuye, the Ouan, and the Houn are only navigable for a very short distance on account of their numerous rapids; neither is there any water-communication between the Menam and the Mekon in Laos or Cambodia, the mountains which separate them forming insurmountable obstacles to the cutting of canals.

On the 24th of June I arrived at Paklaie. The Mekon at this place is much larger than the Menam at Bangkok, and forces its way between lofty mountains with a noise resembling the roaring of the sea and the impetuosity of a torrent, seeming scarcely able to keep within its bed. There are many rapids between Paklaie and Louang Prabang, which is ten or fifteen days' painful travelling. I was tired of my long journey on elephants, and was anxious to hire a boat here, but the chief and some of the inhabitants, fearing that I might meet with some accident, advised me to continue my route by land.

As among the Grisons or the mountains of the Valais, the whole population, who drink the water of the mountain rivulets, are disfigured by immense goitres; but the men are not so subject to them as the women, who rarely escape.

In a letter which I wrote from Cambodia I described the Mekon river as imposing, but monotonous and unpicturesque; but in this part of the country it presents a very different appearance. Where it is narrowest the width is above 1000 metres, and it everywhere runs between lofty mountains, down whose sides flow torrents, all bringing their tribute. There is almost an excess of grandeur. The eye rests constantly on these mountain slopes, clothed in the richest and thickest verdure.

Now, my dear Jenny, let us converse together.[1] Do you know of what I often think when every one around me is asleep, and I, lying wrapped in my mosquito-curtains, let my thoughts wander back to all the members of my family? Then I seem to hear again the charming voice of my little Jenny, and to be listening once more to 'La Traviata', 'The Death of Nelson', or some other of the airs that I loved so much to hear you sing. I then feel regret, mingled with joy, at the souvenirs of the happy—oh, how happy!—past. Then I open the gauze curtains, light my pipe, and gaze out upon the stars, humming softly the 'Pâtre' of Béranger, or the 'Old Sergeant', and thinking that one day I may return Corporal or Sergeant of the battalion of Naturalists.

Perhaps all this does not interest you, but you may feel sure that I do not forget you nor your children; so let me, my dear child, talk to you as we used to talk in the old times as we sat by the fire. When shall we do so again?

In another year, or perhaps two, dear Jenny, I shall think of returning to you all for some time. Shall you be very angry, my dear little sister, when I say that it will be with regret?—for I should wish to visit the whole of the mountains that I can see from my window. I say 'window', but here such a luxury is unknown: I live in a shed without either doors or windows—a room open to every wind.

I would wish, I repeat, to cross the whole network of mountains which extend northward, see what lies beyond them, visit China

---

[1] From here until the words 'Au revoir! Do not forget me' follows the complete text of a letter which Mouhot wrote to his sister in-law on 23 July 1861.

or Thibet, and see the Calmucks or the Irkoutsk. But, alas! I cannot trust my dear insects. I say 'my dear insects' as you would say 'my dear children' to the king of Louang Prabang.

How does all go on at Jersey?—for I hope that you are still there. Your children form your happiness, and you can dispense easily with travelling, or with those people commonly called 'friends'— nothing is so general as the name, or so rare as the reality—and you are right; yet I consider a true friend as a real treasure. I may be wrong, for man is so constituted as always to long for what he has not, but I wish I had friends around me here; these places, now often gloomy, would please me more.

I hoped that at the king's return I should have the happiness of hearing from you; but I am told that his journey will occupy a year, and before that time I shall be away from here.

I hope, my little friend, that all is well with you. Embrace your dear children for me, and talk to them sometimes about their uncle 'Barberousse', who often thinks of them in this distant land, and is collecting stories for their amusement on his return. Ask C—what I shall bring him—a monkey, a sabre to cut off M—'s dolls' heads —no, that would give him warlike ideas, and I do not like our modern soldiers—or a tiger-skin for a carpet. I have several. And your pretty little M—, will she have an ape, a fan, some Chinese slippers (for she must have feet which would be small even in China), some marabout feathers, or a cane to keep her brothers in order?

Adieu, adieu! Au revoir! Do not forget me.

On the 25th of July I reached Louang Prabang, a delightful little town, covering a square mile of ground, and containing a population, not, as Mgr. Pallegoix says in his work on Siam, of 80,000, but of 7000 or 8000 only. The situation is very pleasant. The mountains which, above and below this town, enclose the Mekon, form here a kind of circular valley or amphitheatre, nine miles in diameter, and which, there can be no doubt, was anciently a lake. It was a charming picture, reminding one of the beautiful lakes of Como and Geneva. Were it not for the constant blaze of a tropical sun, or if the mid-day heat were tempered by a gentle breeze, the place would be a little paradise.

You will be happy to hear[1] that I have accomplished this troublesome journey satisfactorily, without the loss of a single man, and without any personal illness. Indeed, my health has been very good, which is more than I can say for my servants, who are so kind and devoted to me. I am even astonished at myself, having gone through the mountainous district which separates the basin of the Menam from that of the Mekon, a place much dreaded by the Siamese, and covered with virgin-forests like those of Dong Phya Phia, without having had a single touch of fever, or, indeed, any indisposition, with the exception of *migraine*, caused by the heat of the sun, and having my feet in a very bad state.

I bless God for the favour granted to me of having accomplished these perilous journeys, and trust wholly to His goodness for the future.

I am now more than 250 leagues north of the place where two years ago I first drank the waters of the Mekon. This immense stream, which is larger here than the Menam at Bangkok or the Thames below London Bridge, flows between high mountains with the rapidity of a torrent, tearing up in the rainy season the trees along the banks, and breaking with a noise like that of a stormy sea against the rocks, which form a number of frightful rapids.

My collections made during the journey are very valuable and beautiful, and I have a great number of new species, both entomological and conchological, with which, if they only reach London

---

[1] This and the next five paragraphs are extracted from Mouhot's letter to his wife started on 27th July 1861.

in safety, our friends will be delighted. All the beautiful kinds that I was asked for, but which elsewhere are so rare that with great trouble I was only able to procure one or two specimens, I have now in great abundance, and also many new sorts. Here I hope to do still better.

My plan is to pass six or eight months of the good season in the neighbouring villages, in order to complete my collection, and next January or March I will try to go north or east, where I shall pass a few more months amidst the Laotian tribes. Probably I shall go no farther, for China would be a barrier to me on the north, and Cochin-China on the east. I shall then return here, and go down the Mekon in July or August 1862, the time when the waters are high, and shall thus reach Korat in a few weeks. I am yet uncertain whether I shall stop there, whether I shall explore the eastern part of the river, or whether I shall go to Cambodia. All my movements depend upon circumstances that may arise. I shall try to profit by all that are favourable, and that will contribute to give interest to my journey.

Do not be anxious when you think of your poor friend the traveller, for you know that up to the present time everything has prospered with him: and truly I experience a degree of contentment, strength of soul, and internal peace, which I have never known before.

XII

LOUANG PRABANG

THE town is built on both banks of the stream, though the greater number of the houses are built on the left bank. The most considerable part of the town surrounds an isolated mount, more than a hundred metres in height, at the top of which is a pagoda.

A beautiful stream, 100 metres wide, unites with the great river to the north-east of the town, and leads to some Laotian and savage villages bearing the name of *Fie*. These are no other than the tribes called *Penoms* by the Cambodians, *Khu* by the Siamese, and *Moi* by the Annamites—all words simply signifying 'savages'.

The whole chain of mountains which extends from the north of Tonquin to the south of Cochin-China, about 100 miles north of Saigon, is inhabited by this primitive people, divided into tribes speaking different dialects, but whose manners and customs are the same. All the villages in the immediate neighbourhood are tributary; those nearest to the town supply workmen for buildings erected for the king and princes, and these are heavily taxed. Others pay their tribute in rice.

Their habitations are in the thickest parts of the forests, where they only can find a path. Their cultivated grounds are to be seen on the tops and sides of the mountains; in fact, they employ the same means as wild animals to escape from their enemies, and to preserve that liberty and independence which are to them, as to all God's creatures, their supreme good.

After waiting for ten days I have at length been presented to the king with great pomp. The reception room was a shed such as they build in our villages on fête-days, but larger and hung with every possible colour. His Majesty was enthroned at one end of the hall, lazily reclining on a divan, having on his right hand four guards squatting down, and each holding a sabre: behind were the princes all prostrated, and farther off the senators, with their backs to the public and their faces in the dust; then in front of his Majesty was your poor brother,[1] dressed all in white, and seated on a carpet, with teacups, basins, and spittoons in silver placed by his side, contemplating this grotesque scene, and having some trouble to preserve his gravity as he smoked his pipe. This visit cost me a gun for the king and various small presents for the princes, for one cannot travel here without being well furnished with presents for the kings, princes, and mandarins. Luckily it is not here as in Siam; the natives are willing to help me, and for a few inches of brass wire I get a beautiful longicorn or some other insect, and these are brought to me on all sides: thus I have succeeded in largely increasing my collection, but five pieces of red cloth have disappeared already.

The day after my first audience I had another from the second king, who wished also for a present. I sought among my stock, which anywhere else would cause me to be taken for a dealer in old stores, and found a magnifying glass and a pair of old-fashioned spectacles with round glasses, which make him look like a gorilla without hair, a little cake of soap (he had great need of it), a bottle of eau-de-cologne, and a bottle of brandy. This last was opened on the spot and duly appreciated. You see all this is expensive, but I am obliged to pay these good people, and the king has been kind to me, and is going to carry my letters for me. It is lucky that he does not understand French; for if at Bangkok the same system of postal curiosity was carried on as was established in Europe by the great king who betrayed La Vallière, I should be hung from the highest tree they could find, without even a warning. I afterwards distributed among the princes some engravings which I had bought

[1] This paragraph and the next are taken from Mouhot's letter to his brother started on 27th July 1861.

at Bangkok—fine Cossack cavalry, lance in rest; some Napoleons
(the First), for which I gave a penny; and some battles of Magenta,
portraits of Victor Emmanuel and of Garibaldi, very white, blue,
and red, and some Zouaves; also some brass-headed nails and some
brandy; and it was quite pleasing to see how delighted they were,
regretting only that I should go away before I had given them my
whole stock.

Alas! what a journey my fragile collection of specimens, so difficult to gather together, has still to take, and what various accidents
may befall them! Those who in museums contemplate the works
of Nature do not think of all the perseverance, trouble, and anxiety
required before they are safely brought home.

15th August, 1861. Nam Kane. A splendid night; the moon
shines with extraordinary brilliancy, silvering the surface of this
lovely river, bordered by high mountains, looking like a grand
and gloomy rampart. The chirp of the crickets alone breaks the
stillness. In my little cottage all is calm and tranquil; the view from
my window is charming, but I cannot appreciate or enjoy it. I am
sad and anxious; I long for my native land, for a little life; to be
always alone weighs on my spirits.

Louang Prabang, 29th August, 1861. My third servant, Song,
whom I had engaged at Pakpriau, begged me to allow him to
return to Bangkok in the suite of the Prince of Louang Prabang,
who was going there to pay tribute. I did all I could do to induce
him to remain with me, but he seemed to have made up his mind
to go; so I paid him his wages, and gave him a letter authorizing
him to receive a further sum at Bangkok for the time occupied by
his return journey.

Same date. Song is gone. How changeable we are! He was always
complaining of cold or had some other grievance, and I cared less
for him than for my other servants—but then I had not had him

long. Yesterday, however, when he asked permission to go, I was vexed. Either he has really suffered much here from illness, or has not been happy with me; perhaps both. I hired a boat to take him to the town, and my good Phrai accompanied him there this morning, and recommended him from me to a mandarin whom I knew. I gave him all that was necessary for his journey, even if it lasts three months, and on his arrival at Bangkok he will receive his money. On taking leave he prostrated himself before me; I took hold of his hands and raised him up, and then he burst into tears. And I, in my turn, when I had bid him farewell, felt my eyes fill, nor do I know when I shall be quite calm, for I have before me, day and night, [a vision of] the poor lad, ill in the woods, among indifferent or cruel people. He has a great dread of fever, and, if he had been taken ill here and died, I should have reproached myself for keeping him; and yet, if it were to come over again, I almost fancy I would not yield to his desire to leave me. May God protect the poor boy, and preserve him from all sickness and accidents during his journey!

In the hamlet of Na-Lê, where I had the pleasure of killing a female tiger, which with its partner was committing great ravages in the neighbourhood, the chief hunter of the village got up a rhinoceros-hunt in my honour. I had not met with this animal in all my wanderings through the forests. The manner in which he is hunted by the Laotians is curious on account of its simplicity and the skill they display. Our party consisted of eight including myself. I and my servants were armed with guns, and at the end of mine was a sharp bayonet. The Laotians had bamboos with iron blades something between a bayonet and a poignard. The weapon of the chief was the horn of a sword-fish, long, sharp, strong, and supple, and not likely to break.

Thus armed, we set off into the thickest part of the forest, with all the windings of which our leader was well acquainted, and could tell with tolerable certainty where we should find our expected prey. After penetrating nearly two miles into the forest, we suddenly heard the crackling of branches and rustling of the dry leaves. The chief went on in advance, signing to us to keep a little way behind, but to have our arms in readiness. Soon our leader uttered a shrill cry as a token that the animal was near; he then commenced striking against each other two bamboo canes, and the men set up wild yells to provoke the animal to quit his retreat.

A few minutes only elapsed before he rushed towards us, furious at having been disturbed. He was a rhinoceros of the largest size, and opened a most enormous mouth. Without any signs of fear, but, on the contrary, of great exultation, as though sure of his prey, the intrepid hunter advanced, lance in hand, and then stood still, waiting for the creature's assault. I must say I trembled for him, and I loaded my gun with two balls; but when the rhinoceros came within reach and opened his immense jaws to seize his enemy, the hunter thrust the lance into him to a depth of some feet, and calmly retired to where we were posted.

The animal uttered fearful cries and rolled over on his back in dreadful convulsions, while all the men shouted with delight. In a few minutes more we drew nearer to him; he was vomiting pools of blood. I shook the chief's hand in testimony of my satisfaction at his courage and skill. He told me that to myself was reserved the honour of finishing the animal, which I did by piercing his throat with my bayonet, and he almost immediately yielded up his last sigh. The hunter then drew out his lance and presented it to me as a souvenir; and in return I gave him a magnificent European poignard.

On my route from B. Nakhau to B. Na-Lê, I spent the night of the 4th of September in a hut at B. Nakone. On the 5th I reached B. Na-Lê, passing through several hamlets. The road lies across high mountains, with jungles full of monkeys uttering their plaintive cries.

20th September. Left B.....p.

28th September.An order was sent to B..., from the council of Louang Prabang, commanding the authorities to prevent my proceeding farther.

15th October. Set off for Louang Prabang.

18th October. Halted at H....

19th October. Attacked by fever.

29th October. Have pity on me, oh my God...!

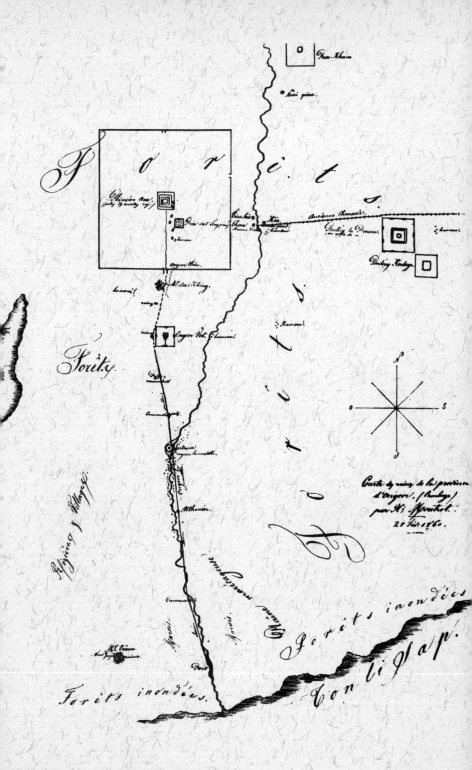

SKETCH MAP OF ANGKOR

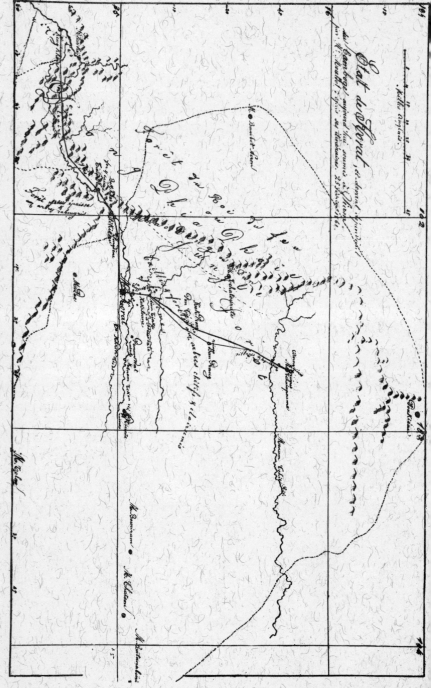

COUNTRY SURROUNDING KORAT IN SIAM

BIBLIOGRAPHY

THE literature on Mouhot himself is sparse, but articles of interest may be found in the *Bulletin de la Societé des Études Indochinoises*, N.S., 36, No. 4, 1961; *Comptes Rendus Mensuels des séances de l'Académie des Sciences d'Outre-Mer*, Tome XXI, November 1961;* and *La Revue Indochinoise*, XXVIII, 11-12, November-December 1925.

The following list of books is intended for the reader who would like to know more about the early exploration of Indochina and also about Angkor.

BASTIAN, Adolph, *The Remains of Ancient Kambodia*, Article VIII, Shanghai (Journal of the Royal Asiatic Society), 1865.

BRIGGS, Lawrence Palmer, *The Ancient Khmer Empire*, Philadelphia, 1955. (Contains a list of seven hundred and fifty books and articles.)

CARPEAUX, Charles, *Les Ruines d'Angkor*, Paris, 1908.

CLIFFORD, Hugh, *Further India*, London, 1904.

COEDÈS, George, *Angkor*, Hong Kong, 1963.

DELAPORTE, Louis, *Voyage au Cambodge*, Paris, 1880.

GARNIER, François, *Voyage d'exploration en Indo-chine*, Paris, 1873.

GITEAU, Madeleine, *Histoire du Cambodge*, Paris, 1957.

GLAIZE, Maurice, *Les monuments du groupe d'Angkor*, Saigon, 1958.

GROSLIER, Bernard-Philippe, *Angkor et le Cambodge au XVIme siècle d'après les sources portugaises et espagnoles*, Paris, 1958.

PAVIE, Auguste, *A la conquête des coeurs*, Paris, 1921.

PYM, Christopher, *The Collapse of the Khmers* (Chapter VI in *Vanished Civilizations*, ed. E. Bacon, London, 1963).

THOMSON, J., *The Antiquities of Cambodia*, Edinburgh, 1867.

For more detailed information the reader is referred to the *Bulletin de l'École Française d'Extrême Orient*, Hanoi-Saigon-Paris (in progress).

* See also *Courrier des Messageries Maritimes*, N.S. 65, November-December 1961.

INDEX

The place-names in brackets provide a link between Mouhot's version and these places as they are more commonly known today. A complete list of place-names mentioned by Mouhot has not been attempted here.